CONTENTS

For the Teacher   1

Jane Austen's Ideology   2

PART 1

Jane Austen's *Pride and Prejudice*   3

PART 2

Jane Austen's *Emma*   37

PART 3

Jane Austen's *Persuasion*   85

Anemones for Miss Austen

Indeed a sweet and knowing lady,
quietly scribbling away her time;
the geographer of a gentle clime
where only the lanes were shady,
the poor kept decently out of sight,
and the neat old-fashioned carriages
manoeuvred the country marriages,
where the curates came off worst, as well they might.

The cool young heroines got their men,
and in due course were suitably wed.
None of the details escaped her pen,
And somehow she never quite said
a word about what happened then,
how they managed with breakfast or bed.

Bernard Bergonzi

Jane Made Plain
Approaches to the Novels of Jane Austen

Pride and Prejudice
Emma
Persuasion

Worksheets devised by
Wendy Jonas

PHOTOCOPIABLE

ISBN 1 876580 78 X

PHOENIX EDUCATION

Jane Made Plain is published by PHOENIX EDUCATION PTY LTD
incorporating St Clair Press.

Sydney
PO Box 3141, Putney 2112
Tel: (02) 9809 3579 Fax: (02) 9808 1430

Melbourne
PO Box 197, Albert Park 3206
Tel: (03) 9699 8377 Fax: (03) 9699 9242

Email: service@phoenixeduc.com
Website: www.phoenixeduc.com

Printing:
Printed in Australia by Five Senses Education, Seven Hills

For the Teacher

◇ The aim of these Worksheets is to provide students with a range of activities which encourage close reading and active engagement with the literature texts. It is not intended that written answers should be produced for every question on every Worksheet but rather that the teacher should plan **a variety of approaches**. Some sections may be used for homework – as preparation for class work or as follow-up and consolidation – and others used in class for student-centred small group work and individual written work as well as teacher-led discussion. Worksheets need not be covered in the given order. It would be advisable, for instance, to cover some parts of Section A (for all novels) after later material.

◇ This approach to literature texts obviously assumes **reading of the whole novel** before close study begins rather than a chapter by chapter examination.

◇ Above all these activities were designed to be **student centred**. Two **group work** tasks are specified for *Pride and Prejudice*.

➤ Worksheet 3 based on the gradual change in the attitudes of Elizabeth and Darcy to one another is designed to help students think about the way Austen presents this central relationship and the fact that the complications do not (as some simplistic discussions imply) end with Darcy's letter. It is suggested that this section should be discussed by all groups with a teacher-led follow-up.

➤ Worksheet 8 D which examines the use of letters as a narrative technique allocates different letters to each group and assumes that time would be allowed for groups to report to the class.

Many of the other questions could also be used to have students reading and talking in small groups. For example, each of the five Houses (Worksheet 1 C) could be allotted to a different group or each group could be responsible for a different character or set of characters (Worksheets 6 or 7).
For *Emma* one **group work** task is specified.

➤ Worksheet 3 allocates a different 'Social Occasion' to each group and assumes that time would be allowed for reporting to the whole class. However, many of the querstions could be used in this way. For example, all groups might discuss the social hierarchy of Highbury and Austen's 'ideology' (Worksheet 2) **or** each of the sections on Emma's errors (Worksheets 4, 5 and 6) could be given to a different group.

For *Persuasion* one major **group work** activity is specified.

➤ Worksheet 5, which traces the misunderstandings of Anne and Wentworth, is designed to focus on the way Austen presents this central relationship from her heroine's point of view but also suggests Wentworth's feelings and reactions. This section is intended for discussion by all groups with a teacher-led follow-up. However many of the questions could also be used to have students reading and talking in small groups. For example, each group could be allocated different Place Settings (Worksheet 2) or 'Sets of People' (Worksheet 3) or Faults of Human Nature (Worksheet 12) with time allowed for reporting to the whole class **or** the *rights and wrongs of Lady Russell's persuasion and of Anne's yielding* (Worksheet 9 Q5) could be debated by all groups and conclusions compared. For *Emma* one major group work task is specified (Worksheet 3). It allocates a different 'Social Occasion' to each group and assumes that time would be allowed for reporting to the whole class. However, many of the questions could be used to have students reading and talking in small groups. For example, all groups might discuss the social Highbury and Austen's 'ideology' (Worksheet 2) or each of the sections on Emma's errors (Worksheets 4, 5, and 5) could be given to a different group.
Page references (for the *Penguin English Library* and *Penguin Classics* editions) are supplied to assist both teacher and students in organising these recommended activities.

◇ The value of **reading aloud** in these groups sections of the novel to which the questions have directed them – or, in the case of direct speech involving a number of characters, of dramatic readings – should be stressed to students.

◇ For each novel a number of **Essay Questions** is supplied. For *Pride and Prejudice* and *Emma* these can be found at appropriate stages of each Worksheet; for *Persuasion* at the end of all the activities.Obviously students would not be able to write every essay in full. Some could be used for discussion, others for planning an essay in outline ie, in point form with examples and quotations selected to illustrate – as a whole class or small group activity or as an individual revision exercise.Classes studying more than one novel can use the Comparison Questions in the same way.

◇ The works of critics whose ideas are referred to or quoted are listed under **Further Reading**. Some approaches for viewing the various **film / TV versions** available are also suggested.

Jane Austen's "Ideology"

Modern critics have pointed to the need to be aware of the 'untold suppositions' of a text, the attitudes and values which constitute its ideology – as revealed for example, by the words with which Chapter 16 of *Emma* opens: ***The hair was curled and the maid sent*** away or by 'absences' or 'silences' (How many references are there in Jane Austen's novels to the poor or to agricultural labourers, the largest single category of workers in her time?)

Wendy Morgan (AATE Conference 1990 – *Investigating Ideology in a Nineteenth Century Text*) suggests asking questions such as:

- What are the concerns of the society, as it is represented in the text?
- How does it function to maintain its social order?
- Where is the power located? Who is excluded from privilege?
- What movement within the social order is possible?

The 'self-evident truths' or assumptions of the society presented in Austen's novels may seem clear but what is her own attitude to this society? Was she a conventional member of her class, unquestioningly accepting its position and ideology? or was she *perfectly able to see with absolute clarity the defects of the world she used* (Mark Schorer)?

A selection of different readings:

- Kettle sees her acceptance of class structure as a limitation but praises her *understanding of and feeling about the position of women in society*, a concern he calls *subversive*; in the reading of the feminist critics Gilbert and Gubar *she always defers to the economic, social and political power of men* and the submission of even her lively, independent heroines in the endings *reinforces women's subordinate position in a patriarchal culture.*
- Christopher Gillie, examining how in the world of the novels society sets constraints on the individual, claims that *what is shown to be essential is that the personal should take priority over the social, not the other way round;* however Vivien Jones finds in most of the novels *a defence of the established social order and of society's claims over the individual* (but in ***Persuasion*** a much less conservative attitude to society and an openness to social change.)

A biographer's viewpoint

For how much it is possible to know from research outside the novels of Jane Austen's attitudes to such things as politics, women's rights, religion, see pp139-141 of Claire Tomalin's interesting biography, *Jane Austen: A Life.*

Sections of each worksheet related to aspects of the novel's 'ideology':

Pride and Prejudice	*Emma*	*Persuasion*
Worksheet 1 – Part A, Part B, Essay question 3	Worksheet 1	Worksheet 1
Worksheet 2 – Essay Q 7 & Q 8	Worksheet 2 – Q3, Q4	Worksheet 2 – Q 1 (b)
Worksheet 3 – Q 1 (h) and (j)	Essay Question 6	Worksheet 3 – Q e (i)
Worksheet 4 – Essay Question 12		Worksheet 10
Worksheet 6 – Q 2 (e)		Worksheet 11 – Q 4
Worksheet 7 – Essay Question 15		Essay Questions 5 & 6

Jane Austen's

Mr Darcy, you must allow me to present this
young lady to you as a very desirable partner.

"Pride and Prejudice"

Pride and Prejudice – Contents

Section A:	**Setting**	**5**
Worksheet 1	The World of the Novel	6
Section B:	**Themes / Issues / Main Concerns**	**9**
Worksheet 2	Courtship and Marriage	10
Worksheet 3	The Importance of Correct Judgement	12
Worksheet 4	Elizabeth's Struggle for Individuality and Self-Respect	16
Worksheet 5	Follies and Nonsense	17
Section C:	**Characters: Simple and Intricate**	**19**
Worksheet 6	Heroine, Hero and Villain	20
Worksheet 7	Characters Continued	23
Section D:	**Narrative Methods**	**25**
Worksheet 8	Narrative Methods	26
Suggestions for Further Reading and Viewing		**32**

Section A: SETTING

Worksheet 1
The World of the Novel

A. The Society of Which the Novel Gives a Picture

1. Jane Austen's world (the English countryside of the late 18th and early 19th Century) was very different from the world of the late 20th / early 21st Century. To appreciate the attitudes and values of the society depicted in her novels, particularly the limitations imposed upon women, background reading in some of the following is recommended:

   ➤ Fay Weldon *Letters To Alice: On First Reading Jane Austen*
      (in the form of letters by a modern 'feminist' novelist to an imaginary niece with green spiked hair.)
   ➤ David Cecil *A Portrait of Jane Austen*
      (particularly *Prologue: The World* and illustrations eg, portraits, pictures of houses).
   ➤ Oliver MacDonagh *Jane Austen – Real and Imagined Worlds*
      (a professional historian analyses Austen's life and considers her treatment of the same subjects and ideas in her novels – See Chapter 2 *The Female Economy* and Chapter 4 *Girlhood*).
   ➤ Susan Watkins *Jane Austen's Town and Country Style*.
   ➤ Claire Tomalin *Jane Austen: A Life*.
   ➤ G M Trevelyan *A Social History of England* Volume IV.

2. In your reading of the novel itself be ale rt to details which throw light on the following:
   ➤ The class system / the importance of property ("the landed gentry").
   ➤ Insistence on manners and decorum eg, visiting code, forms of address, dancing etiquette, female behaviour.
   ➤ Pastimes: visiting, balls, card-playing and other games / female accomplishments
   ➤ Marriage as a social ***connexion*** – considerations of birth, family, money.
   ➤ The need for a 'good' marriage for a girl without property or social standing
   ➤ Attitudes to 'fallen' women.
   ➤ Transport and communication
   ➤ The post / the importance of letters

B. Jane Austen's Attitude To Her World

Serene Acceptance or "Regulated Hatred"?

Many readers and critics have found in Jane Austen's presentation of the relationships of the everyday social life of her time an acceptance of the values of her world and an amused and good-natured tolerance of the foibles and weaknesses of human nature. Richard Church says *"The basis of Jane's work is serenity"* but D W Harding warned against *"supposing that a mind like hers ... found the ordinary social intercourse of the period congenial and satisfying".*

He argued in an early essay titled 'Regulated Hatred; An Aspect of the Work of Jane Austen' that Austen has been misread as *"a delicate satirist"* and that her novels were rather a way of dealing with her reactions to *"things and people which were to her, and still are, hateful"* and in his later Introduction to the Penguin edition of *Persuasion* that *"The older idea that her novels simply offered amusing entertainment for people like those she lived amongst (and their successors down to our own time) has given way to the recognition in her work of a much stronger dislike of the society in which she seemed comfortably embedded, a dislike often implicit, often conveyed in passing and easily ignored, occasionally intense and bitter..... The urbanity, the charm, the wit and lightness of touch, the good humour, are there... but.... for full enjoyment we have to appreciate a more complex flavour."*

a) How would you sum up the novelist's attitude to the society she depicts in *Pride and Prejudice* as a whole?

b) In particular consider the "flavour" or tone of the following sections of the novel in which she shows gossip, rumour or **report** at work in that world:

References:
Chapter 3, from **and a report soon followed** to **most disagreeable man in the world.**
Chapter 48, from **All Meryton seemed striving** to **the appearance of his goodness.**
Chapter 50, from **The good news quickly spread** to **her misery was considered certain.**
Chapter 55, last paragraph – beginning **The Bennets were speedily pronounced.**

C. Houses.

What is the importance of each of the following in the novel? Consider associated characters and plot incidents and any other uses which Jane Austen makes of each setting.

a) the Bennet house, Longbourn
b) Netherfield Park
c) Hunsford Parsonage
d) Rosings
e) Pemberley

ESSAY QUESTIONS

1. *In the discussion of fiction, the term 'setting' may refer to descriptions of localities, landscapes, and interiors. It may, however, refer to period as well as place, and to social convention. 'Setting' may express (directly or indirectly) the main concerns of a work of fiction.*

   Discuss the function of 'setting' in the presentation of Jane Austen's main concerns in **Pride and Prejudice.**

2. ***"Three or four families in a country village is the very thing to work on."***
   (Jane Austen in a letter to her niece.)

   What uses does the novelist make of such seemingly limited material in **Pride and Prejudice**?

3. *"In **Pride and Prejudice** Jane Austen portrays the life and values of her society with a marvellous fidelity but she does not sufficiently question them."*

   Show whether you agree with this statement, making close reference to the novel to support your argument.

4. D W Harding disagrees with readers who find in Austen's work *"no more than delicately entertaining studies of the surface of polite society and its trivial doings amid the costumes and architecture of advertisers' Regency"*.

   Do you find anything more than this in **Pride and Prejudice**?

Section B:
THEMES/ISSUES/
MAIN CONCERNS

Worksheet 2
Courtship and Marriage

1. **Passage for Close Reading:** Chapter 1

   Marriage is indicated as one of the main concerns of the novel in the first chapter. How? Consider the following:

   a) The opening sentence.
      Jane Austen's use of irony – tone of phrase *a truth universally acknowledged*? Incongruity of what follows?

   b) The dialogue or conversation that comprises most of the chapter after this opening. (This lends itself to a dramatic reading. In **groups** of three, read this chapter aloud, taking the roles of Mrs Bennet, Mr Bennet and the narrator who makes authorial comment. Then discuss the following:
      - Early in the conversation Mr Bennet's contributions are given in reported or indirect speech. Effect created?
      - What is revealed of each character by the content and characteristics of his or her speech (ie, by what they say **and** how they say it)? In particular which sections of the dialogue demonstrate the qualities summed up in the concluding paragraph of authorial comment – Mrs Bennet's *mean understanding* and Mr Bennet's *mixture of quick parts* (intelligence), *sarcastic humour, reserve and caprice*?
      - What tone is indicated for the novel to follow – serious or light-hearted and comic? ironic or straightforward?)

   c) The reinforcing of the idea of marriage in the final sentence.

2. What attitudes to marriage are shown by the following characters?
   Charlotte (chapters 6, 22, 32)
   Mr Collins (chapters 15, 19, 20, 22, 23)
   Mrs Gardiner (chapters 26, 27)
   Wickham (chapters 27, 35, 39, 49, 52)
   Colonel Fitzwilliam (chapter 33)
   Lydia (chapters 47, 51, 52)
   Mrs Bennet (chapters 1, 20, 49, 55, 59 and throughout)
   Lady Catherine (chapter 56)
   Jane (chapter 59)
   Elizabeth (chapters 6, 19, 22, 24, 26, 27, 30, 34, 42, 39, 49, 50, 51, 56, 59)
   Mr Darcy (chapters 8, 34, 35, 58)
   Mr Bennet (chapter 59)

Almost as soon as I entered the house I singled you out as the companion of my future life.

3. *"Marriage... is the concern of all her novels – right marriage and wrong marriage, the right and wrong reasons for marrying."* (Norman Sherry)
    Which of the following are presented as good marriages and which as unsatisfactory?
    ✶ Mr and Mrs Bennet   ✶ Mr and Mrs Gardiner
    ✶ Charlotte Lucas and Mr Collins   ✶ Lydia Bennet and Mr Wickham
    ✶ Jane Bennet and Mr Bingley   ✶ Elizabeth Bennet and Mr Darcy
    Give detail from the novel with page or chapter references to support your opinions.

After dinner she went to show her ring and boast of being married.

ESSAY QUESTIONS

5. Give an account of the three proposals of marriage which Elizabeth receives in **Pride and Prejudice**. Analyse her reactions to each and what is revealed of the character and attitudes of the gentlemen concerned.

6. *"A novel about marriage and money."*
    Is this an adequate description of **Pride and Prejudice**?

7. **"Your lively talents would place you in the greatest danger in an unequal marriage.....My child, let me not have the grief of seeing you unable to respect your partner in life."** (Mr Bennet to Elizabeth Chapter 59.) Use this conversation from towards the end of **Pride and Prejudice** as the starting point for a discussion of the views of marriage presented in the novel as a whole.

8. The poet W H Auden wrote of Jane Austen
    "It makes me feel uncomfortable to see
    An English spinster of the middle-class
    Describe the amorous effects of 'brass',   'brass' = slang for 'money'
    Reveal so frankly and with such sobriety
    The economic basis of society."
    To what extent do you think the novel as a whole endorses the attitudes of the money-minded society Austen depicts?

Worksheet 3
The Importance of Correct Judgement

1. Group Work

> **Note:** The original title chosen by Jane Austen was *First Impressions*. In the novel Elizabeth and Darcy form first impressions of one another distorted on both sides by **pride** and **prejudice**. This leads to **misunderstandings** and **conflicts**. The gradual change in Elizabeth's attitude to Darcy and his to her is presented through situations and dialogue rich in **ambiguity** and **irony** which should be obvious on a second reading.
>
> With the ideas **highlighted in bold** in mind, re-read the sections of the novel indicated and discuss the questions.

a) Describe the situation in which Elizabeth and Darcy form their first impressions of one another. (Ch 3, Ch 4)

b) Trace their relationship through its conflicts and misunderstandings to the stage where Darcy proposes to Elizabeth. (Chapters 6, 8, 10, 11, 18, 28, 30, 31, 32, 33, 34.) In particular, how has her prejudice against him been reinforced immediately before the proposal?

c) i) What does Darcy's letter reveal to Elizabeth about her own prejudice and / or pride? (Ch 35, Ch 36, Ch 37.) Comment in detail on the ***contrariety of emotion*** the letter produces, ie, on her immediate and later reactions.

   ii) *She has learned much from the letter, very much indeed, but Jane Austen is too perceptive a reader of character to suppose that all comes clear at once...... nor, though Elizabeth does know herself henceforth much better, does she know herself completely.* (Andrew H Wright) In the light of this critical comment can you find any irony in her reflections in the paragraph in Chapter 36 beginning ***"How despicably have I acted!"***?

Jane Made Plain: *Pride and Prejudice*

d) After her first **perturbed state of mind** subsides Elizabeth tells herself that **His attachment excited gratitude, his general character respect; but she could not approve him; nor could she for a moment repent her refusal, or feel the slightest inclination ever to see him again.** (Chapter 37.) Consider her reactions when she does do so in the unexpected encounter at Pemberley: (Ch 43.)

> What is the importance of the conversation with Mrs Reynolds and her **earnest contemplation** of the portrait?

> How does Jane Austen suggest the complexity of Elizabeth's feelings during and after the meetings with Darcy?

> What is the significance of Darcy's behaviour to Mr and Mrs Gardiner?

e) What change in herself does Elizabeth acknowledge as she reflects on Darcy's visit with his sister? (Ch 44) Nevertheless does your reading support that of Andrew H Wright who finds in this section *the continued resistance which she is still putting up against the release of her own strong feelings*?

f) At the same time as Jane Austen focuses on Elizabeth's not very clear feelings she presents Darcy's behaviour in Derbyshire from the viewpoint of other characters: Mr and Mrs Gardiner (Chapter 44); Miss Bingley (Chapter 45).
How does this influence your reading of these episodes ?

g) i) How and why does Elizabeth misread Darcy's behaviour when she is forced to leave Derbyshire? (Chapter 46). Explain the irony of situation in her awareness that **never had she so honestly felt she could have loved him.**

   ii) How is this irony reinforced through Elizabeth's conflicting emotions in Chapters 48, 50 and 52 ?

h) R G Geering points out that to maintain tension and interest before the reconciliation Jane Austen makes use of the social environment which *allowing few chances for meeting alone, restricts their attempts to reach an understanding of one another* and Penny Gay that the first meeting after Derbyshire is *in Elizabeth's home (with all its attendant disadvantages).* Examine from this point of view:

   i) Darcy's visit to Longbourn in Chapter 53 which prompts Elizabeth's vexed question at the beginning of the next chapter **"Why, if he came only to be silent, grave and indifferent, . . . did he come at all?"** (See Ch 60)

   ii) The tensions and frustrations of the dinner party in Chapter 54.

i) Despite her refusal to be intimidated by Lady Catherine in Chapter 56 Elizabeth's **discomposure of spirits** is still stressed at both the beginning and end of the next chapter. Why does she feel this way ?

j) Penny Gay says that *Austen keep (s) to the powerless woman's point of view as the story moves to its end.* With this in mind comment on the following word choices applied to Elizabeth at the beginning of Chapter 58: *"a desperate resolution", "boldly", "courage".* Does she challenge decorum by actually proposing to Darcy?

k) To sum up:

i) *Darcy is proud,without doubt, but the real concern of the novel is to show how Elizabeth comes to change her first impressions and to re-cast her idea of pride.* (R G Geering)

To consider this idea, trace all the references to **pride** throughout the novel which lead up to the following:

"We all know him to be a proud, unpleasant sort of man; but this would be nothing if you really liked him."

"I do, I do like him," she replied with tears in her eyes, **"I love him. Indeed he has no improper pride."** (Chapter 59)

References: Ch 3, p58; Ch 5, pp 66-7; Ch 11, p102; Ch 14, p111; Ch 16, pp124-5, p127; Ch 25, p180; Ch 33, p219; Ch 34, p221, p223, p225; Ch 36, p233, p236; Ch 43, p271, p278; Ch 44 p281, p285; Ch 52, p338; Ch 58 pp 377-8, Ch 59, pp 384-5.

(Alternate references Penguin Classics Edition: p12, pp19-20, p51, p58, p70, p72, p121, pp154-5, p157,159. 160, p168, 171, p204, 210, p212, 216, p263, p297, p303.)

ii) What is the importance of the Jane / Bingley romance in the development of Elizabeth's and Darcy's relationship?

(See also Section D Narrative Methods Worksheet 8.)

iii) What role has Lady Catherine played in ending the misunderstanding between Darcy and Elizabeth?

What a pleasantly ironic invention it is that Darcy, who has alienated Elizabeth by interfering in her sister's affairs, and is by no means ready to repent his interference, should be roused to indignation and action when Lady Catherine tries to interfere in his. (Mary Lascelles)

(NB The Olivier film completely changes Lady Catherine's motives and character. See **Suggestions For Reading and Viewing**)

2. Elizabeth's prejudice stems from a pride in her own perceptions.
   - Find all the evidence you can from the novel which suggests she does have the ability to judge people and situations well.
   - Apart from Darcy, what **two** mistakes does she make in judging people ? What warnings or clues does she ignore ?

ESSAY QUESTIONS

9. Discuss how the progress of Elizabeth's relationship with Darcy illustrates and explores several of the important themes in *Pride and Prejudice*.

10. *"Reading the novel, we may reasonably begin by attributing pride to Darcy, and prejudice created by that same pride to Elizabeth, but we quickly learn that each has a share of both qualities."* (Norman Page)
    Discuss, making close reference to specific sections of the novel to support what you say.

11. *"How despicably have I acted !," she cried; "I, who have prided myself on my discernment ! I, who have valued myself on my abilities! –"* (Chapter 36)

    Is Elizabeth in fact a poor judge of character? In your answer, consider her judgement of Darcy and of at least three other characters in the novel.

Worksheet 4
Elizabeth's Struggle for
Individuality and Self-Respect

> Consider what the novel shows of the position of women, the constraints placed on female behaviour by the rules of social decorum, and the possibilities of happiness for an intelligent woman in such a society.

Some ideas/sections of the novel related to this are listed to get you started. Find other examples of your own.

- R G Geering's point that Elizabeth *takes her place so naturally in the social milieu that we might overlook her increasing isolation as the story progresses.*
- Charlotte's discussion with Elizabeth in Chapter 6 of the strategies a woman must use for **fixing him** (a man)
- The entail and the way it affects the prospects of Elizabeth and her sisters (Mr Collins's reminder Chapter 19)
- Bingley's sisters' criticism of the independence and **want of decorum** shown by Elizabeth in walking to visit Jane with **her petticoat six inches deep in mud** (Chapter 8)
- The ideal **accomplished woman** discussed by Miss Bingley and Darcy (Chapter 8) – Elizabeth's attitude.
- Lady Catherine's interrogation of Elizabeth about her sisters' education and social position (Chapter 29)
- Charlotte's acceptance of the *inferior rating .... granted by a money-minded society incapable of appreciating her intelligence* (Yasmine Gooneratne) and Elizabeth's *continuous refusal to accept such a valuation of herself.*
- The social restrictions which frustrate Elizabeth in the later chapters.
(See Question 1. (h) and (j) on Worksheet 3)

ESSAY QUESTIONS

12. Discuss the proposition that *"What makes Elizabeth a worthy heroine is her twofold struggle — to achieve self-knowledge through an understanding of her feelings towards Darcy and to reconcile her desires with the demands of society."* (R G Geering)

13. Discuss in relation to *Pride and Prejudice* D W Harding's thesis that Jane Austen's early novels deal with the "Cinderella theme" in which *"the heroine is in some degree isolated from those around her by being more sensitive or of finer moral insight or sounder judgement, and her marriage to the handsome prince at the end is in the nature of a reward for being different from the rest and a consolation for the distresses entailed by being different."*

Worksheet 5
"Follies and Nonsense . . ."

"I hope I never ridicule what is wise and good. Follies and nonsense, whims and inconsistencies do divert me, I own, and I laugh at them whenever I can." (Elizabeth to Darcy Chapter 11)

"The more I see of the world, the more I am dissatisfied with it; and every day confirms my belief of the inconsistency of all human characters, and the little dependence that can be placed on the appearance of either merit or sense." (Elizabeth to Jane Chapter 24)

What **characters** and **episodes** in the novel illustrate the following faults of human nature?

   ★   snobbery and condescension

   ★   flattery; obsequiousness

   ★   mercenary motives, materialism

   ★   conceit, self-importance, pomposity

   ★   obtuseness and stupidity

   ★   shallowness and frivolity

   ★   malice; spitefulness; jealousy

   ★   insincerity, duplicity, hypocrisy

   ★   gossip / relishing the misfortunes of others

Any others?

ESSAY QUESTIONS

14. *"Follies and nonsense do divert me and I laugh at them whenever I can."*
How does Jane Austen reveal such a response to the world in *Pride and Prejudice*?

Section C:
CHARACTERS:
SIMPLE & INTRICATE

Worksheet 6
Heroine, Hero and Villain

1. Elizabeth

a) The following is a suggested list of character traits or qualities revealed in Austen's characterisation of her heroine:
   ★ vibrant, lively personality; vitality and energy
   ★ intelligence; confidence in her own judgements and perceptions
   ★ refusal to be intimidated by rank and wealth, snobbery and condescension
   ★ outspokenness; independence
   ★ capacity for articulate speech and witty repartee
   ★ ability to laugh at herself and others
   ★ honesty, willingness to admit mistakes
   ★ values and standards which set her apart from her family and those in her social world

Can you add any others ?

Consider the various methods of characterisation used by Jane Austen set out below. Draw up a table with two columns headed **Character Trait** and **Method of Characterisation**. Find at least one section of the novel which illustrates each of Elizabeth's listed qualities and in the second column indicate which method is used to reveal it. (Include as many methods as possible but note that for Elizabeth there is no character sketch.)

Methods of Characterisation
* brief character sketch / authorial comment
* "character in action" ie, how the character behaves in specific plot incidents.
* attitudes or comments of other character(s)
* reactions to / relationships with particular characters
* dialogue or conversation
* correspondence
* implied judgement i.e. conveyed indirectly by narrator's tone eg, irony **or** humour.

b) Geering points to what he sees as an interesting aspect of Austen's characterisation: *that Elizabeth, despite what she says, is unconsciously attracted to Darcy early in their relationship but is unable to admit this even to herself.* As evidence of this "psychological insight" he firstly offers Elizabeth's deliberately provocative behaviour towards Darcy (*perverse but unrecognized signs of real interest*) and secondly interprets the embarrassment she often feels about the behaviour of her family in Darcy's presence as an unconscious *fear that he might come to despise her.*

Re-read and discuss these sections of the novel and any others which might support or refute this view.

2. Darcy

Elizabeth Bennet is a complicated and penetrating heroine; the two men with whom she associates herself romantically must also be intricate and intelligent. (Andrew H Wright)

a) Some readers have not found Darcy 's characterisation successful, especially the changes he is made to undergo.

   i) Consider R G Geering's claim that *Jane Austen gives us two Darcys, instead of one.....It is hard to believe that the man who behaves with such exemplary politeness and forbearance in the second half of the book would have been capable of that famous insult at the Netherfield ball.* *
   (* actually the Meryton assembly)

   ii) On the other hand
      ➢ E M Halliday argues that Austen's technique of giving the reader direct insight into Darcy's mind in the early stages of the novel (see Chapters 6–12) is preparing respect and sympathy for him *despite his snobbish behaviour, partly because we know he is falling in love with Elizabeth. Since we have begun to like her very much ourselves, this stands to his credit in the face of her prejudice; it shows his discrimination.* **and**
      ➢ Reuben A Brower[1] has demonstrated in the irony and ambiguity of many of the dialogues between Elizabeth and Darcy *the double presentation of Darcy's character* ie: the possibility of a more pleasant interpretation of his behaviour than Elizabeth's **blind, partial, prejudiced** view. (See Chapters 6, 10, 11, 18)
   What do you think ?
   Does the character develop convincingly OR are there "two Darcys"?

b) Darcy's relationship with Bingley is one method used to present his character.
   Find evidence in the novel for what Andrew H Wright calls *the solidity of temperament implied in his affection for Bingley.*

c) Consider carefully the way Miss Bingley is used to influence our response to Darcy. (Chapters 6, 8, 9, 10, 11, 12, 18, 45)

d) What function does his sister Georgiana serve in the characterisation of Darcy? (Chapters 16, 35, 44, 45)

e) Elizabeth is usually thought of as the character who shows independence or individuality in the novel's world of rigid conventions and class divisions. Consider however the following comments:

   Darcy's offer of marriage to Elizabeth, greatly his social inferior, is in fact a courageous challenge to social convention (R G Geering)

   His affection and respect for Elizabeth are extended later to the Gardiners, who, like her, defeat the expectations of society... in spite of their trading connections. (Yasmine Gooneratne)

---

1   Read the whole essay. **Light and Bright and Sparkling: Irony and Fiction in *Pride and Prejudice*.**

3. Wickham

"His appearance in the story comes just as Elizabeth, smarting from Darcy's disapprobation, willingly abrogates her critical faculties in favour of a pleasant countenance and manner." (Andrew H Wright)

Mr Denny entreated permission to introduce his friend.

a) Read Chapters 15-16 noting the stress on Wickham's handsome appearance and conversational skills. Examples?
   (Compare Darcy: ***I am ill qualified to recommend myself to strangers*** (Chapter 31))

b) Underneath his charming surface Wickham is calculating and dishonourable.
   What clues are there for the reader even in these early chapters?
   What evidence from later sections of the novel reinforces this?

c) What is Wickham's motivation in his conversations with Elizabeth in Chapter 41 and Chapter 52? (Elizabeth's?)

d) Consider Wickham's behaviour after his marriage to Lydia. (Chapters 51, 52 53).
   What do you think Mr Bennet means when he says ***"I defy even Sir William Lucas himself to produce such a valuable son-in-law"*** (Chapter 53) and calls Wickham his favourite over Darcy and Bingley at the end of Chapter 59? (See also end of Chapter 57)

Worksheet 7
Characters Continued

A. The Use of Characters as Foils

1. Discuss the way the first character in each of the pairs listed below is used to highlight qualities of the second.
   a) Jane[1] / Elizabeth
   b) Charlotte / Elizabeth
   c) Bingley / Darcy
   d) Wickham / Darcy
   e) Mr Bennet / Elizabeth

2. Characters related to both Elizabeth and Darcy are balanced in significant ways:

   a) Compare the behaviour of Elizabeth's relations (Chapters 9, 18) with that of Darcy's aunt (Chapters 29, 31, 56.)

   b) From this point of view what is the function of Mr and Mrs Gardiner / Colonel Fitzwilliam and Georgiana Darcy?

B. The Comic Characters

1. *"What incomparable noodles she exhibits for our astonishment and laughter!"*
   (G H Lewes in 1859)

   Each of the characters listed below is used by Jane Austen to provide humour and/or treated satirically.

   For each in turn draw up a table of **Character Traits / Methods of Revealing Them** as in Question 1 (a) Worksheet 6
   a) Mrs Bennet
   b) Mr Bennet
   c) Mr Collins
   d) Lady Catherine
   e) Lydia

2. Marvin Mudrick calls the minor comic characters Mary Bennet and Sir William Lucas *"single-postured simpletons"*. We might also add Bingley's brother-in-law, Mr Hurst, who appears briefly in Chapters 7, 8, 10, 11. What is the single character trait of each? Give quotations or detail and page references to illustrate.

   You must come and make Lizzie marry Mr Collins !

1   Eighteenth century meaning of **candour** = generosity, kindliness, sweetness of temperament (see Chapter 4).

C. Simple or Intricate?

> *"It does not necessarily follow that a deep, intricate character is more or less estimable than such a one as yours..... but intricate characters are the most amusing."* (Elizabeth to Bingley Chapter 9)

Which of the characters mentioned in this Worksheet would you categorise as **simple** (fixed and predictable, lacking complexity or self-awareness) and which as **intricate** (variable, capable of contradictory motives but also self-aware, intellectually and emotionally complex)?

ESSAY QUESTIONS

15. Tony Tanner delights in **Pride and Prejudice** as *"a novel in which the brightness and sparkle of the heroine's individuality are not sacrificed to the exacting decorums or the manipulative persuasions of the social group. Elizabeth Bennet says she is humbled, but we will always remember her as laughing."*
    With this comment as a starting point, discuss Jane Austen's presentation of her heroine.

16. *"It might be argued that Darcy is the least successful character in* **Pride and Prejudice** *and the book's one major flaw."* (R G Geering) Do you agree ? Make close reference to the novel to support your point of view.

17. *"Although Elizabeth and Darcy dominate* **Pride and Prejudice**, *minor characters are also important for the development of the novel's themes."*
    Discuss this view, considering at least three of the following:
    Mr Bennet; Mrs Bennet; Charlotte Lucas; Mr Collins; Miss Bingley;
    Lady Catherine; Lydia.

18. Many readers place Jane Austen's "fools" among the most richly comic characters in English literature; others call them caricatures or grotesques, too exaggerated to be true to life.
    Discuss your response to the characterisation of at least **two** of the comic characters in **Pride and Prejudice**.

19. *"For what do we live but to make sport for our neighbours, and laugh at them in our turn."* (Mr Bennet to Elizabeth Chapter 57)
    "I hope I never ridicule what is wise and good. Follies and nonsense, whims and inconsistencies do divert me, I own, and I laugh at them whenever I can." (Elizabeth to Darcy Chapter 11)
    Discuss the similarities and differences in the characterisation of Elizabeth and her father and the importance of their relationship in the novel as a whole.

20. *"Interplay of character in Jane Austen's novels generally takes place through dialogue rather than incident"*. (Norman Sherry)
    Select **three** of the following conversations and examine the way character is revealed through dialogue:
    Chapters 5; 9; 11; 14; 16; 18 (Elizabeth and Darcy); 24; 31; 56; 59 (Elizabeth and Mr Bennet).

Section D:
NARRATIVE
METHODS

Worksheet 8
Narrative Methods

A. The Structure of the Plot

1. Analysing Jane Austen's plot construction in **Pride and Prejudice**, Mary Lascelles found a *pattern... formed by diverging and converging lines, by the movement of two people who are impelled apart until they reach a climax of mutual hostility, and thereafter bend their courses toward mutual understanding and amity.* Dorothy Van Ghent used this idea to construct the following diagram *which shows the relationship of correspondence-with-variation between the Darcy-Elizabeth plot and the Bingley-Jane sub-plot, the complication of the former and the simplicity of the latter, the successive movements toward splitting apart and toward coming together, and the final resolution.*

   a) Examine the diagram's representation of the Jane-Bingley relationship. Draw a larger version and mark on it significant stages (incidents / specific chapters) in the process of *"splitting apart"* and *"coming together"*. What reason can you suggest for the *"simplicity"* of this sub-plot (See Worksheet 3. Question k (ii))

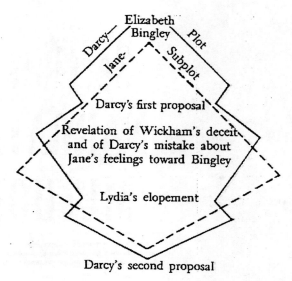

   b) Consider the more complex plot.
      Add to sections of the novel shown on the diagram chapter numbers and other key incidents related to the *"splitting apart"* and *"coming together"* of Elizabeth and Darcy.

2. *Even while they are drawing yet further apart, Elizabeth and Darcy have begun to feel unfamiliar doubts; sure as each still is of his and her own critical judgement, both have come to question the standards of their own social world.* (Mary Lascelles)

   a) In Chapter 36 Elizabeth admits to herself that Darcy's criticism of her family is a **mortifying, yet merited reproach**. How has this view of her relations been prepared for from early in the novel and especially in Chapter 18?

   b) Darcy also learns that the manners of his world – as represented by his aunt and Miss Bingley – can be criticised.
      Which sections of the novel illustrate this? Details? Chapter References?

3. One way in which Austen makes the reader *anticipate, with delicious anxiety, that Elizabeth will wind up in Darcy's arms* (E M Halliday) is to establish early in the narrative grounds for doubting her prejudices against him.

   a) One of her strongest prejudices is her belief that Darcy has deliberately ruined Jane's happiness. The conversation with Charlotte in Chapter 6 prepares for Darcy's answer to this accusation in Chapter 35. How?

   b) How is the reader prepared for her discovery that she has been wrong about Darcy's treatment of Wickham? Details? Chapter References?

4. Halliday says the plot creates suspense which *"depends mostly on our waiting for Elizabeth to discover two things: that Darcy is in love with her; and that she is in love with Darcy. The reader must be led to suspect both of these things before Elizabeth does, or the suspense is lost."*

   a) By what methods does Jane Austen provide clues that Darcy is falling in love with Elizabeth? (See Chapters 6, 7, 8, 9, 10, 11, 12, 18, 30, 31, 32, 33.
   Also Worksheet 6: Question 2 a (ii))

   b) In the light of the idea that Elizabeth is unconsciously attracted to Darcy (See Worksheet 6 Question 1b) consider her opinion of Miss De Bourgh on their first meeting at the end of Chapter 28, her reaction to the news that Darcy is expected at Rosings in Chapter 30, and her thoughts in Chapter 31 in the paragraph beginning **Elizabeth looked at Darcy to see how cordially he assented to his cousin's praise**.
   Can you detect any **irony** in the narrator's tone?

B. Style . . . Language / Humour / Irony

Jane Austen's narrative technique involves more than simply plot construction. In order to be aware of the **tone** of her authorial voice, of *what the aloof, sceptical, didactic presence who tells her stories wants us to think of the people and events* (Donald J Gray), it is important to look closely at her use of language – the **irony** in a seemingly simple or factual statement; the **wit** in the choice or placing of a single word.

Discuss the following examples and find others of your own:

➤ *They . . . were in the habit of spending more than they ought, and of associating with people of rank; and were therefore in every respect entitled to think well of themselves and meanly of others.* (Chapter 4)

➤ *Mr Collins had only to change from Jane to Elizabeth – and it was soon done – done while Mrs Bennet was stirring the fire.* (Chapter15)

➤ *Mr Wickham was so perfectly satisfied with this conversation that he never again . . .* etc. (Chapter 53)

➤ *Mrs Bennet's many cheerful prognostications of a bad day* (Chapter 5) or *querulous serenity* (Chapter 42)

➤ *The visitors to Rosings were all sent to one of the windows to admire the view* (Chapter 29)

➤ *Lady Lucas's enquiring. . . . after the welfare and poultry of her eldest daughter* (Chapter 39)

➤ *Miss Bingley's congratulations were all that was affectionate and insincere* (Chapter 60)

C. Dialogue

> *In the novel as a whole, we are overwhelmed by the wealth and liveliness of the dialogue; conversations carry the story smoothly and swiftly along, illuminating character and incident, bringing Elizabeth, especially, to vivid life.* (Yasmine Gooneratne)

a) In pairs (or small groups when other characters are present) **dramatise** the following verbal encounters between Elizabeth and Darcy: Chapter 8, Chapter 10; Chapter 18; Chapter 31, Chapter 32; Chapter 34; Chapter 58; Chapter 60.
   Which of these conversations, apart from revealing character, forward the plot or have any other narrative function ?

b) Select **three** other conversations (eg, from those listed in Essay Question 20 on Worksheet 7 or Worksheet 2 Question **1** or examples of your own choice) and explain how *they "carry the story along"*.
   Note the **tone** created in many of these conversations by the interplay of direct speech and the narrator's comment.

c) Explain how Lydia's silly chatter in Chapter 39 prepares for future plot developments.

d) **Passages for Close Reading**
   The two passages listed below deal with conversations during Elizabeth's visits to Rosings but these conversations are presented more by indirect or reported speech than in direct speech / dialogue.

   i) end of Chapter 29 from ***When the gentlemen had joined them, and tea was over, the card tables were placed*** . . .

   ii) Chapter 31 – from ***The invitation was accepted of course*** to ***and made no answer***.

   Analyse Jane Austen's language and style in each passage, commenting in particular on the narrative method – use of direct or reported speech, arrangement of ideas, word choice, sentence structure, and tone.

D. The Use of Letters

Whether or not, as has been speculated, the original version was in epistolary form ie, narrated as a novel-in-letters, **Pride and Prejudice** uses a large number of letters and refers frequently to other correspendence not quoted directly.

a) ***"My stile of writing is very different from yours"*** (Darcy to Bingley Chapter 10)
   Discuss the contrast in their characters implied in the discussion of their contrasting approaches to letter-writng.

b) Darcy's letter after Elizabeth's rejection of his proposal is crucial to the development of the plot. Discuss the view of Mary Lascelles that it is a *"not quite plausible"* plot mechanism – *The manner is right but not the matter: so much, and such information would hardly be volunteered by a proud and reserved man.*

c) **Group Work**

Read and discuss the letters allocated to your group and prepare a report for the class:

Do they forward the plot or prepare for later plot developments? Do they reveal character? or Both?

Is the language straightforward or is a humorous, satirical or ironic tone created?

- ➤ Ch 7:   Miss Bingley's letter to Jane and Jane's letter to Lizzie from Netherfield
- ➤ Ch 13:   Mr Collins's letter to Mr Bennet announcing his visit to Longbourn
- ➤ Ch 21:   Miss Bingley's insincere letter to Jane about departure for London
- ➤ Ch 24   second letter from London
- ➤ Ch 26:   Jane's letters from London – finally admitting to
             having been entirely deceived by Miss Bingley
- ➤ Ch 35:   Darcy's letter to Elizabeth after her rejection of his proposal
- ➤ Ch 46:   Jane's letters to Elizabeth about Lydia's elopement
- ➤ Ch 47:   Lydia's letter to Colonel Foster's wife, read by Jane and Elizabeth
- ➤ Ch 48:   Mr Gardiner's letter from London about the search for Lydia and
             Wickham; Mr Collins's letter 'consoling' Mr Bennet for Lydia's sinful
             behaviour
- ➤ Ch 49:   Mr Gardiner's news from London ***They are not married*** /
             Wickham's debts, plans for marriage
- ➤ Ch 50:   Further letter from Mr Gardiner – proposed visit of
             Lydia and Wickham to Longbourn
- ➤ Ch 51:   Elizabeth's request for information from Mrs Gardiner
             about Darcy's presence at Lydia's wedding
- ➤ Ch 52:   Mrs Gardiner's reply
- ➤ Ch 57:   extracts from Mr Collins's letter to Mr Bennet about Jane, Lydia, and
             rumours of Elizabeth's marriage
- ➤ Ch 60:   Elizabeth's joyful letter to her aunt Gardiner about her forthcoming
             marriage; Mr Bennet's letter to Mr Collins announcing the marriage of
             Elizabeth and Darcy
- ➤ Ch 61: Mrs Wickham's letter to Mrs Darcy

"You write uncommonly fast"

To Sum Up:

In the light of the following critical comments review Jane Austen's narrative methods:

A Walton Litz: *The first half of the novel could easily be translated into a play; here Darcy and Elizabeth are 'on stage', joining with the other characters to dramatize the novel's psychological and social conflicts. Howard S Babb has shown how Jane Austen plays on the word 'performance' in the early dialogues, bringing all the implications of the word together in the great scene at Rosings, where Elizabeth's actual performance at the piano becomes the centre of a dramatic confrontation. But after the scene at Rosings, when Darcy's letter begins Elizabeth's movement toward self-recognition, the term 'performance' quietly disappears from the novel. The first half of the novel has indeed been a dramatic performance, but in the second half a mixture of narrative, summary, and scene carries the plot toward its conclusion.*

Tony Tanner: *In essence a letter is written and read in retirement from the social scene... By combining the dramatic and the epistolary modes, Jane Austen has deftly set before us a basic truth – that we are both performing selves and reflective selves. It is in her social performance that Elizabeth reveals all her vitality, vivacity and wit..; it is in private reflection . . . that she matures in judgement, reconsiders her first impressions...... How suitable then, that after giving us some of the most brilliant 'performances' in English fiction, Jane Austen should allow her novel to move away from performance towards reflection after Darcy's letter. She thus subtly offers an analogue of how – in her view – the individual should develop. For if the human being is to be fully human, then to the energy of performance should be added the wisdom of reflection.*

ESSAY QUESTIONS

21. *"All works of fiction tell a story, but what sets them apart is the particular way in which the story is told."*
    Discuss the narrative methods used by Austen in *Pride and Prejudice* and what these methods enable her to achieve.

22. *"What is character but the determination of incident ? What is incident but the illustration of character?"*
    How does Jane Austen's narrative art in *Pride and Prejudice* illustrate this assertion by Henry James ?

23. Discuss A C Bradley's claim that our pleasure in reading Jane Austen lies in the fact that she *"regards her characters, good and bad alike, with ironical amusement, because they never see the situation as it really is and as she sees it."*

24. *"Darcy and Elizabeth's courtship evolves through fifteen major dialogues, taking place in three different locations under vastly different conditions"* (Penny Gay) Discuss the importance of this dialogue for the novel as a whole.

25. *"Much as I abominate writing I would not give up Mr Collins's correspondence for any consideration"* (Mr Bennet in Chapter 57)
    Discuss the correspondence between Mr Collins and Mr Bennet and what these letters contribute to the novel.

26. **Passage for Close Reading**
    Read carefully the following passage from Chapter 60 of *Pride and Prejudice*
    (from *"Shall you ever have the courage to announce* – to *earnest desire of being loved by her sister.*)
    Write an essay on Jane Austen's language and style and the appropriateness of these to this stage of the novel.
    Comment on such things as vocabulary, sentence structure and tone and assess the effectiveness of her narrative techniques

Suggestions for Further Reading and Viewing

Reading

The following critical works are referred to in this order in the worksheets.

Richard Church   *The Growth of The English Novel* Methuen 1957

D W Harding   *'Regulated Hatred: An aspect of the work of Jane Austen'* (in *Jane Austen: A Collection of Critical Essays* ed. Ian Watt Prentice Hall 1963)

D W Harding   Introduction to Penguin English Library edition *Persuasion* 1966

D W Harding   *'Jane Austen and Moral judgement'* (in *The Character of Literature from Blake to Byron Pelican Guide To English Literature* 5 ed Boris ford 1957)

Norman Sherry   *Jane Austen* Evans Brothers 1966

Andrew H Wright   *Jane Austen's Novels: A Study In Structure* Chatto & Windus 1961

R G Geering   *"Pride and Prejudice": The Comic Muse* (a lecture for the English Association at the University of Sydney May 1981)

Penny Gay   *Jane Austen's "Pride and Prejudice"* Horizon Studies in Literature series Sydney University Press / Oxford 1990.)

Mary Lascelles   *Jane Austen and Her Art* Oxford University Press 1939

Yasmine Gooneratne   *Jane Austen* Cambridge University Press 1970

Norman Page   *The Language of Jane Austen* Basil Blackwell 1972

E M Halliday   *Narrative Perspective* in *"Pride and Prejudice"* (in *Norton Critical Edition* ed Stephen M Parrish W W Norton & Co, 1972)

Reuben A. Brower   *'Light and Bright and Sparkling: Irony and Fiction in "Pride and Prejudice"'* (in *Jane Austen: A Collection of Critical Essays* ed Ian Watt above.)

Marvin Mudrick   *'Irony As Discrimination: "Pride and Prejudice"'* (in *Jane Austen: A Collection of Critical Essays* ed Ian Watt above.)

Tony Tanner   Introduction to Penguin English Library edition *Pride and Prejudice 1972*

Dorothy van Ghent   *The English Novel: Form and Function* Harper and Row, NY 1953

Other Recommended Works

Sandra M Gilbert}   *Jane Austen's Cover Story* (in *The Madwoman In The Attic: The Woman*
& Susan Gubar }   *Writer & the Nineteenth Century Literary Imagination*) Yale Uni Press 1979
Claudia L Johnson   *Jane Austen: Women, Politics and The Novel* Uni of Chicago Press 1988
Robert Gard   *Jane Austen 's Novels*: The Art of Clarity Yale University Press 1992
Ivor Morris   *Jane Austen and The Interplay of Character* Athlone Press 1999
J B Priestley   *The English Comic Characters* (essay on Mr Collins) Bodley Head 1925

Viewing

> ◇ FILM directed by Robert Z Leonard for MGM 1940 with Greer Garson as Elizabeth and Laurence Olivier as Mr Darcy. Available on Video.
>
> ◇ BBC (Granada) TV SERIES 1985 screenplay by Fay Weldon, directed by John Glenister with Elisabeth Garvie as Elizabeth and David Rintoul as Mr Darcy. Available at ABC Shops and on Video.
>
> ◇ BBC TV SERIES 1995 screenplay by Andrew Davies, directed by Simon Langton with Jennifer Ehle as Elizabeth and Colin Firth as Mr Darcy. Available at ABC Shops and on Video.

The old black-and-white film made in 1940 is still shown and much loved, perhaps for its combination of Greer Garson and Laurence Olivier early in their careers.

1. Note the anachronistic Victorian crinolines for the women's costumes

2. Olivier's comments are interesting:
   "I was very unhappy with the picture. It was difficult to make Darcy into anything more than an unattractive-looking prig and darling Greer seemed to me all wrong as Elizabeth"
   Discussion could examine
   - how successfully he portrays the Darcy presented by Jane Austen
   - whether the screenplay allowed Garson to be the Elizabeth of the novel, (requiring her, for example, at the garden party which replaces the ball at Netherfield to respond to Miss Bingley's spiteful comments by weeping and to be comforted by Darcy to a background of romantic music).

3. Olivier commented further *"I also thought that the best points in the book were missed"*.
   Certainly the film makes numerous changes to the novel's plot – eg:
   - an opening carriage race showing the rivalry between Mrs Bennet and the Lucases
   - Wickham is at the Meryton assembly before Darcy appears with Bingley / Darcy's insult is changed and he does ask Elizabeth to dance / she refuses and dances with Wickham.
   - Darcy rescues Elizabeth from a comic pursuit by Mr Collins (at the garden party in place of the Netherfield ball)
   - Elizabeth weeps again to poignant music after Darcy's proposal
   - Darcy writes **no letter** but since the elopement of Lydia and Wickham follows immediately after his proposal **(no visit to Pemberley)** comes to Elizabeth's home to explain the Wickham / Georgiana episode.
   - Mr Collins's letter to Mr Bennet is replaced by a visit in which he speaks his *"condolences"* to Mrs Bennet and is reprimanded by Charlotte.
   - Lady Catherine's interview with Elizabeth at Longbourn reveals Darcy's kindness to Lydia, and is followed by Darcy's being told by his aunt (in the carriage in which he waits outside) *"She's right for you, Darcy!"* (the American academic Claudia L Johnson speaks of Lady Catherine's metamorphosis into *a swell old gal.*[1])
   - In the ending Kitty and Mary have suitors as well as Jane and Elizabeth.
   Were the best points in the book missed? Do any sections of the film express Austen's main concerns or capture the novel's tone (as examined in Worksheets 2, 3, 4.)

---

1   In an article on the film *Mansfield Park* in *The Times Literary Supplement* December 1999.

Both TV Series, originally screened as 5/6 weekly instalments of approximately one hour, are long and detailed, including much of Jane Austen's dialogue and most of the key plot episodes.

For either version discussion could examine:

1. how well some of the following **important scenes** are realised
   - the balls – Darcy's insult at the Meryton assembly / Elizabeth's refusal to dance at Lucas Lodge / Elizabeth dancing with Darcy at Bingley's ball
   - Elizabeth at Netherfield – arrival with muddy petticoat / interaction with Darcy and Miss Bingley
   - the proposals – Mr Collins and Mr Darcy
   - the scenes at Rosings
   - the surprise meeting of Darcy and Elizabeth at Pemberley / the role of Miss Bingley in this section
   - Lady Catherine's visit to Longbourn

2. **Performances / Casting**
   - Comic and / or minor characters:
     - ✦ Mrs Bennet
     - ✦ Mr Collins
     - ✦ Lydia
     - ✦ Mary
     - ✦ Lady Catherine
     - ✦ Mr Bennet
     - ✦ Charlotte
     - ✦ Miss Bingley
     - ✦ Mrs Gardiner
   - How well is Elizabeth's vitality and independence suggested?
   - Is Wickham's charm and duplicity conveyed?
   - Does the actor playing Darcy avoid the charge of some critics that there are "two Darcys" in the novel?

3. the way Austen's **narrative techniques** are **translated to the visual medium** of television:
   - the authorial voice (The famous opening sentence is handled differently in each version)
   - the use of letters
   - irony – of situation as well as in the tone of the narrative
   (eg: Is Elizabeth's misreading of Darcy's reactions at the news of Lydia's elopement – and elsewhere – conveyed?)

If time permits the viewing of both versions, all the above could be used for comparisons.

4. Additions / Alterations:
(The intention in examining such details is to focus on Jane Austen's main concerns and careful structuring of her plot)

Fay Weldon's adaptation (1985 Series)
- dramatising of Mr Collins' proposal to Charlotte
- Charlotte's wish to inform Elizabeth before betrothal announced
- Mr Collins's 'acquatic hat' for planting bullrushes
- Elizabeth's "There are few people whom I really love" speech to Wickham not to Jane
- Elizabeth's reaction to Wickham and Miss King given to younger sisters and in letter to Charlotte with Charlotte rather than Mrs Gardiner passing judgement on Wickham's mercenary behaviour
- Elizabeth's reaction to news of Lydia's elopement – running to Pemberley and bursting into Darcy's drawing room (rather than as in the novel Darcy's walking in on her distress at the Inn)

Andrew Davies's adaptation (1995 version)
- Elizabeth introduced out walking, then starting to run as if revelling in her freedom.
- Darcy's 'physicality' – fencing, riding, shooting, playing billiards, swimming
- Darcy in his bath at Netherfield
- Lydia's meeting Mr Collins on the stairs in her underwear
- Darcy up all night writing his letter to Elizabeth
- Darcy's wet shirt and informal dress after bathing in the lake at Pemberley just before encountering Elizabeth
- content of Mr Collins's letter changed
- scenes of Lydia and Wickham in London
- Wickham saying to Elizabeth *"You must despise me"*
- omission of dinner party at Longbourn (Ch 54)
- scene in which Darcy admits concealing Jane's visit to London and tells Bingley *"Go to it!"*

Some 'modern' readings of the 1995 series:
- Andrew Davies has said that he intended Elizabeth's long, solitary walks throughout his screenplay to suggest her releasing all her pent up sexual energy.[1]
- *Colin Firth's Darcy is often framed or entrapped by windows, adding extra layers to his social and sexual frustration, as when he watches Elizabeth, on the other side of the glass, frolicking with a dog.*[2]

Davies's Ending
- double wedding – with shots of various characters at particular words of marriage ceremony:
  (*carnal lusts* = Mr and Mrs Bennet,
  the procreation of children = Lady Catherine and her daughter,
  to avoid fornication = Lydia and Wickham;
  mutual society, help and comfort = Elizabeth and Darcy)
  (See Worksheet 2 – Courtship and Marriage Q2.)

---

1   **Andrew Davies at Winsconsin summary** by Anna G on Republic of Pemberley website 24/5/2001.

2   From a review of **Jane Austen in Hollywood**, Hambledon Press, 1999 on Jane Austen Society Australia website.

Jane Austen's "Emma"

Emma – Contents

Section A:	**Setting and Social Occasions**	**39**
Worksheet 1	The Society of Which the Novel Gives a Picture	40
Worksheet 2	Emma's Little World – Hartfield and Highbury	41
Worksheet 3	Social Occasions	44
Section B:	**Emma's Errors**	**51**
Worksheet 4	The Harriet Smith – Mr Elton Affair	52
Worksheet 5	The Jane Fairfax – Frank Churchill Affair	54
Worksheet 6	Humiliation – and Self-Awareness?	57
Section C:	**Mainly Males**	**61**
Worksheet 7	The Men in Emma's Life	62
Section D:	**Emma as a Comic Novel**	**65**
Worksheet 8	The Definition of Comedy	66
Worksheet 9	The Comic Characters	69
Worksheet 10	Comedy Continued	71
Section E:	**Austen's Irony**	**73**
Worksheet 11	Revision Exercise	74
Suggestions for Further Reading and Viewing		**76**
Addendum	**Alternative Page References**	**83**

Section A:
SETTING &
SOCIAL OCCASIONS

Worksheet 1
The Society of Which the Novel Gives a Picture

1. Jane Austen's world (the English countryside of the late 18th and early 19th Century) was very different from the world of the late 20th/early 21st Century. To appreciate the attitudes and values of the society depicted in her novels, background reading in some of the following is recommended:
   - David Cecil, *A Portrait Of Jane Austen* (particularly *Prologue: The World* and illustrations, for example portraits, pictures of houses, etc.)
   - Fay Weldon, *Letters To Alice: On First Reading Jane Austen* (in the form of letters by a modern 'feminist' novelist to an imaginary niece with green spiked hair).
   - Oliver MacDonagh, *Jane Austen – Real And Imagined Worlds* (a professional historian analyses Austen's experiences and considers her treatment of the same subjects and ideas in her fiction. See in particular Chapter 6 *Social Traffic*).
   - W A Craik, *Jane Austen In Her Time*.
   - G M Trevelyan, *A Social History Of England* Volume 1V.
   - Claire Tomalin, *Jane Austen: A Life*.

2. In your reading of the novel itself be alert to details which throw light on the following:
   - The class system /birth, rank and family tradition/the importance of property ("the landed gentry").
   - Polite society's disapproval of earning one's living in 'trade'/movement within the social order.
   - Marriage as a social connection – considerations of money, birth and family.
   - Insistence on manners and decorum, eg: visiting code, forms of address, dancing etiquette, female behaviour.
   - The position of women/female accomplishments/attitudes to a woman's having to work – governesses.
   - Attitudes to illegitimacy.
   - Pastimes: visiting, card-playing and other games, music, balls.
   - Transport and communication.

A Barouche. A fashionable style of vehicle favoured by smart ladies such as Mrs Elton.

Worksheet 2
Emma's Little World – Hartfield and Highbury

*"The scene never moves from Highbury, and though some of the characters come and go, Emma never leaves home for more than a few hours. The important things are not what happens **to** her but what happens **in** her."*
(Elizabeth Drew)

"What, indeed, is Emma to do with her abundant energy and lively mind in a place as small and unchallenging as Highbury?"
(Penny Gay)

1. The setting is Highbury, a village in Surrey[1] situated sixteen miles from London, and Jane Austen makes us aware of the smallness of this world, of the way the life of this little country community is concentrated within itself.

   a) Without modern means of travel and communication the distance from London seems much greater. Consider:
      i) Mr Woodhouse's concern about the fatigue of horses and coachman at the beginning of Chapter 11.
      ii) Reactions to Frank Churchill's *"travelling sixteen miles twice over"* to have his hair cut (chapters 25, 26).

   b) Read the description in Chapter 27 of what Emma sees as she looks out from Ford's shop (beginning *"Much could not be hoped from the traffic of even the busiest part of Highbury"*). What atmosphere is created?

2. Consider the importance of what Emma in Chapter 7 calls *"the tittle-tattle of Highbury"*:

   "We listen to the buzz of gossip about the arrival of Mrs Elton; the visit of the fashionable young man, Frank Churchill; the mysterious gift of the pianoforte to Jane Fairfax; the scandal of the secret engagement."
   (Elizabeth Drew)

   a) Identify chapter/page references for the gossiping referred to in the above quotation.

   b) Explain the irony in the gossip repeated by Harriet to Emma at the end of Chapter 8.

   c) What news spread around Highbury so quickly in Chapter 53?

   d) What effect(s) does Jane Austen create by making gossip and rumour so much a part of her social setting?

"It passed to Mrs Cole, Mrs Perry, and Mrs Elton" (Chapter 53)

---

1   See Ronald Blythe's Note to the 1966 Penguin edition under the heading **Topography** p469 and **a map of the world** in Penny Gay's *Jane Austen's "Emma"* pp2-6.

---

3. The social arrangement of the village is hierarchical, reflecting the class structure of the wider society:

The Social Hierarchy of Highbury

The group highest in "fortune and consequence" [1]
(below the aristocracy and above the commercial bourgeoisie):
Mr Knightley of Donwell Abbey and the Woodhouses of Hartfield.

The second level:
the vicar; the female relations of his predecessor, Mrs and Miss Bates; Mr Weston; and the newly rich Mr Cole (fortune from 'trade' / ten years in Highbury before entry into polite circles).

The third rank – not so clearly delineated:
the attorney, Cox; the apothecary, Perry; probably Mrs Goddard and her schoolmistresses and the tenant farmer, Robert Martin and his family.

Below these: (briefly mentioned only)
the shopkeeping class; the landlady of the Crown; the servants; the poor.

Despite the apparently unquestioning acceptance of this social order, we should not automatically conclude that an attitude of one of her characters is the same as Jane Austen's.

For example, which of the following does the narrator seem to endorse?

How is your reading influenced? eg: by direct comment / the narratorial voice?
by the choice of language and tone?
by the use of other characters?

- Ch 4, Emma's attitude to **the yeomanry** (ie: farmers – the class to which Robert Martin belongs)
- Ch 8, Mr Knightley's claim that Mr Martin is Harriet's superior
- Ch 16, Emma's disapproval of Mr Elton's **so well understanding the gradations of rank below him and be(ing) so blind to what rose above.**
- Ch 19, Emma's dislike of visiting the sociable Mrs and Miss Bates because of **all the horror of being in danger of falling in with the second rate and third rate of Highbury, who were calling on them forever.**
- Ch 25, Emma's attitude to an invitation from the Coles
- Ch 36, Mrs Elton's **horror of upstarts** and attitude to the Tupman family from Birmingham
- Ch 42, Mrs Elton's **raptures** over Jane's prospective employer, **a lady known at Maple Grove. Delightful, charming, superior, first circles, spheres, lines, ranks, every thing...** .
- Ch 46, Mrs Weston's comment on Frank's proposed marriage: **It is not a connexion to gratify.**
- Ch 47, Harriet's attitude to **the disparity** between herself and Mr Knightley.

1 Emma's words in Chapter 16. See this chapter for information on the two families.

Jane Made Plain: Emma

4. In his poem 'Anemones for Miss Austen', Bernard Bergonzi calls Jane Austen...

the geographer of a gentle clime
where only the lanes were shady,
the poor kept decently out of sight.

Passage for Close Reading:

One of the few references in her novels to the lower ranks of society is the brief episode in Chapter 10 in which Emma and Harriet make a ***charitable visit*** to the poor cottage in Vicarage Lane.

Read this passage carefully (from ***They were now approaching the cottage*** to ***the gentleman joined them***) and consider the following:

Arnold Kettle says that *Harriet's silly responses underline most potently the doubt that Emma herself feels as to the adequacy of her own actions. There can be no point in this passage (for it has no inevitable bearing on the plot), save to give a sense of the darker side of the moon, the aspect of Hartfield that will not be dealt with –* and concludes that *the doubt in the reader's mind that an essential side of Hartfield is being conveniently ignored – is not entirely answered.... one's doubts... are in fact, like Emma's, swept away by the arrival of Mr Elton and the plot.*

a) Is one point of the passage to provide an ironic tone at Emma's expense?
   ➢ Consider her words ***I feel now as if I could think of nothing but these poor creatures all the rest of the day and yet who can say how soon it may all vanish from my mind?***
      How soon does it vanish? Why?
   ➢ What is on her mind for the rest of the chapter? (Is the tone serious or comic?)

b) Do you as a reader share Kettle's uneasiness that the serious issue of poverty seems to be glossed over?

Worksheet 3
Social Occasions

The novel presents six main social events which Jane Austen uses very cleverly, making one emphasise another.

1. Group Work

Read closely and discuss the social occasion assigned to your group.

Your report for the rest of the class might include any of these general points you consider relevant and any ideas suggested by the specific details supplied for each group.

- What this social event reveals of customs and etiquette, the social code of the time.
- The significance of this occasion in the light of earlier events and / or later plot developments.
- Austen's characterisation in this small episode – individual characters / character groupings and contrasts.
- What is revealed and / or concealed by what is said and done – underlying tensions and feelings suggested.
- Comic and ironic effects.
- Serious issues or moral values stated or implied.

Group 1: The Westons' Christmas Dinner

Ch 13: significance of Harriet's absence – Emma's manipulations and Mr Elton's behaviour / reaction to her brother-in-law's advice – *the blunders which often arise from a partial knowledge of circumstance* / humour in John Knightley's eccentric attitude to this social occasion – contrast with Mr Elton.

Ch 14: opening – manners and social decorum / Mr Elton's behaviour and Emma's *effort ... to preserve her good manners* / topic of conversation before, during and after dinner / custom of women moving into drawing room after dinner – Mr Woodhouse's joining them / Emma's relationship with Mrs Weston.

Ch 15: Mr Elton's continued *improprieties* – Mrs Weston's *surprise* and Emma's *reproof* / characteristic behaviour of various characters in the little crisis which brings this social occasion to a close / how this leads to situation of Emma and Elton alone in one carriage for journey home / effect of *drinking too much of Mr Weston's good wine* on Mr Elton / Emma's *fewer struggles for politeness* as journey proceeds / how this social occasion ends.

Ch 25: Read carefully the section from ***The Coles had been settled for some years in Highbury –*** to ***poor comfort***. and consider the two critical comments that follow:

> *The ambiguous way in which such a description fluctuates between an apparently impersonal statement of fact, and Emma's prejudiced and snobbish reaction, leaves one slightly uncertain about the attitude that one is supposed to take towards the Coles* (Frank Bradbrook)

> *... an ironic moment of social agony for Emma when it seems that she and her father, alone in all Highbury, stand too high to be invited* (Oliver MacDonagh)

Note the attitudes of Mr Knightley and the Westons to the Coles' invitation / Emma's quick change of heart.

Ch 26: tone of ***She meant to be very happy in spite of the scene being laid at Mr Cole's*** / Emma's comment on Mr Knightley's arriving ***like a gentleman*** and his reaction (reason for use of carriage later revealed?) / Frank Churchill's close attentions to Emma c.f. little details of his behaviour to Jane Fairfax / much discussed topic of mysterious gift of a piano from London; attitudes of various characters including Jane's reaction and Emma's indiscreetly confided suspicion; reminder of Frank's sudden visit to London / tone of comment on ***the usual rate of conversation*** at such social events (from ***a few clever things*** to ***– heavy jokes***) / Emma's reaction to Mrs Weston's idea about Mr Knightley and Jane Fairfax – self-deception? (link between concern here for ***little Henry*** and later reference in Ch 33?) / Emma's mimicking of Miss Bates – foreshadowing of a later occasion? / comparison of Emma's and Jane's playing and singing / Mr Knightley's attitude to Frank / how does this social occasion end? (link between Frank Churchill 's last words and beginning of Chapter 29)

Ch 27: Emma's self-congratulation on ***her condescension in going to the Coles***. Yet she is ***not quite easy***. Why?

Group 3 The Dinner at Hartfield

Ch 34: influence of the social code – obligation to hold a formal dinner at Hartfield for Mrs Elton despite Emma's dislike of the newcomer (See previous Chapters 32, 33) / reasons for absence of Harriet and inclusion of Jane Fairfax / significance of the conversation about Jane's wet walk to the post office — reason for her **blush, quivering lip** and **tear**?; Emma's judgement about the source of the letters; characteristic reactions of other characters / custom of new bride leading into dinner – Mrs Elton's attitude.

Ch 35: after dinner: Mrs Elton's presumptuous attitude to Jane (parallels with Emma?) / Jane's reference to the **governess-trade** (link with reasons for delaying her departure from Highbury?) / Mrs Elton's interpretation of Mr Woodhouse's joining the women c.f. the Westons' dinner (Group 1) / the anti-social John Knightley and the sociable Mr Weston / Emma's reactions to news of Frank Churchill's return

Ch 36: social comedy in the long conversation between Mr Weston and Mrs Elton / Mrs Elton's criticism of the Tupmans of Birmingham (a centre of trade and commerce) – compare Emma's attitude to the Coles (Ch 25)

Group 4: The Ball at the Crown Inn

Ch 29: tone of narrator's opening comments on dancing; **Frank Churchill had danced once in Highbury** (where?) **and longed to dance again** (with whom? See end of Ch 26) / Emma's own motives and her interpretation of Frank's / humour in serious discussion of trivial details during the planning; Mr Woodhouse's character / Frank's reason for consulting Miss Bates?

Ch 30: Jane Fairfax's animated response – link with her later headache? / Mr Knightley's attitude – possible readings?

Ch 38: detail of customs at balls – supper, card playing, etiquette of asking Mrs Elton to lead the dancing; style of dancing / Mr Weston's character – echo of Ch 36? / Frank Churchill's **odd humour** / Mrs Elton's vanity and egotism / evidence of Emma's unconscious attraction to Mr Knightley? / Mr Elton's deliberate insult to Harriet – his wife's reaction / Mr Knightley's **leading Harriet to the set** – link with Chs 40 & 47? Emma and Mr Knightley drawing closer?

Dancing the quadrille.

Group 5: Mr Knightley's Strawberry Party

Ch 42: Planning and preparation – Mrs Elton and Mr Knightley / descriptive details of Donwell Abbey – Emma's respect for it as *the residence of a family of true gentility* and pleasure in the grounds – *English verdure, English culture, English comfort* – also Austen's attitude? traditional image of the well-tended country estate and the responsible landowner? (cf. Pemberley in *Pride and Prejudice*); *I am sick of England* Frank Churchill / characterisation: Mr Weston's cheerful unawareness of Mr Knightley's feelings; Mr Woodhouse; Mrs Elton (Jane Austen's method of suggesting her incessant and egotistical babble?) / Frank Churchill's delayed arrival, Mrs Elton's behaviour to Jane Fairfax and her hasty departure – *Oh Miss Woodhouse, the comfort of being sometimes alone!* – possible explanation? change in Emma's attitude to her / Mr Knightley's *tête-à-tête* with Harriet and Emma's reaction (links with Chapters 40 & 47?) / Frank's late appearance (whom did he meet as he came to Donwell?) / Emma's explanation of his cross mood, plan to go abroad and reluctance to join outing to Box Hill next day? other possible reading? (See Chapter 50)

Group 6 The Picnic at Box Hill

Ch 43: Opening paragraph – contrast between *the outward circumstances. □ in favour of a pleasant party* and the social disharmony established immediately / the moods and motives of various characters: why is Frank at first *silent* and *dull* then *gay and talkative*? (reminder of Chapter 42?); why does Emma flirt with Frank and act in a *gay and thoughtless* way? Is her rudeness to Miss Bates linked to this?; why is Mrs Elton put out?; what hidden meanings may be found in the dialogue between Jane Fairfax and Frank Churchill?; why does Jane ask her aunt to join Mrs Elton? why does Mr Knightley follow?; what are the moods or feelings of Frank and Emma just before the carriages arrive? / why does Emma say that of the other *seven silent people* the only two whose thoughts she would not fear to know are Mr Weston and Harriet? / evidence that Emma still hopes to match Harriet and Frank? / how does Mr Knightley's behaviour to Emma contrast with Frank's? / how does this social occasion end?

Ch 44: after the picnic: Emma's reaction as she reflects on her own behaviour? / evidence that Frank's behaviour has pushed Jane Fairfax to breaking point? (See also Chapters 45, 46, 48, 50 and 52)

Ch 45: reason for Mr Knightley's sudden departure for London? (See Chapter 49) / irony of Mr Woodhouse's **unjust** praise of Emma's visit to Miss Bates and significance of Mr Knightley's reaction?

Ch 52: malice in Mrs Elton's reference to Box Hill – context? what **secret** does she think Emma does not know? what does **she** not know? (irony)

2. Writing Task

Imagine you are each of the following characters in turn:

a) **Mrs Elton / Harriet Smith / Mr Woodhouse** after the visit to Donwell Abbey.

b) **Jane Fairfax / Frank Churchill / Mr Knightley** after the picnic to Box Hill.

In at least one paragraph for each character, give your thoughts and feelings about this day and recent events.

NOTE: *In this task you need to change the point of view from that in the novel; to vary your language and style by using an appropriate register for the character you are re-creating; and to show understanding of the novel's plot, characters, relationships, and main concerns*

3. Games

As well as the main social events, beginning with the backgammon table from which Mr Knightley rescues Emma in Chapter 1, activities such as the playing of cards and word games, charades and riddles are frequently presented.

a) List all the examples you can find of such pastimes. Chapter / Page references?

b) Several critics have found a link between these 'trivial pursuits' and the serious issues of the novel.

Consider how the following different readings all use the 'games' metaphor or motif:

► *Games of all sorts – verbal games, parlour games, the games of social behaviour – are a continual theme in Emma's life, and in the novel that tells her story . . . Frank Churchill . . . is of course the novel's most consummate game-player.* Penny Gay

► *Ultimately (Emma) must realise that she has viewed life as a game in which she can display her imagination and powers of perception; it is no accident that Jane Austen uses Emma's fondness for conundrums, charades, and word-games to reveal her errors of imagination. This particular motif culminates early in the third volume in a scene *at Hartfield. (*Ch 41. See Worksheet 5 Q 8)* A Walton Litz

► *What she cannot forgive, of course (See conclusion of Ch 20) – is not that Jane may have been playing games with the affections of two other people, but that she refuses to contribute to Emma's game.* Christopher Gillie

► *Frank and Emma's game is flirtatious; Frank and Jane play a more serious game and have more at stake.* Jennifer Gribble

► *Emma and her friends believe her capable of answering questions which puzzle less quick and assured girls, an ability shown to be necessary in a world of professions and falsehoods, puzzles, charades and riddles. But word games deceive especially those players who think they have discovered the hidden meanings, and Emma misinterprets every riddle. ... The civil falsehoods that keep society running make each character a riddle to the others, a polite puzzle. With professions of openness Frank Churchill has been keeping a secret that threatens to embarrass and pain both Emma and Jane Fairfax. Emma discovers the ambiguous nature of discourse that mystifies, witholds, coerces, and lies as much as it reveals.* Sandra M Gilbert & Susan Gubar

Essay Questions Linked to Worksheets 1, 2 and 3

1. *In the discussion of fiction, the term 'setting' may refer to descriptions of localities, landscapes and interiors. It may, however, refer to period as well as place, and to social convention. 'Setting' may express (directly or indirectly) the main concerns of a work of fiction.*
   Discuss the function of setting in the presentation of Jane Austen's main concerns in *Emma*.

2. What are the functions in *Emma*, apart from forwarding the plot, of **three** of the following:
   the portrait painting; the Westons' Christmas dinner party; the ball at the Crown Inn; the alphabet word game; the strawberry party at Donwell Abbey; the picnic at Box Hill?

3. In Kipling's story, *The Janeites*, one of the characters complains of Jane Austen's novels:
   'Twasn't as if there was anythin' to 'em either. I know, I had to read 'em. They weren't adventurous, nor smutty, nor what you'd call even interestin' — all about girls o' seventeen (they begun young then, I tell you), not certain 'oom they'd like to marry; an' their dances an' card-parties an' picnics, and their young blokes goin' off to London on 'orseback for 'air-cuts an' shaves."
   How would you defend *Emma* against this criticism?

4. *"It is as a portrait of female life among ladies in an English village fifty years ago that **Emma** is to be known and remembered."* (Anthony Trollope 1865)
   Is this your reading, well over a hundred and fifty years later?

5. ***"Three or four families in a country village is the very thing to work on"*** (Jane Austen).
   What uses does Jane Austen make of this small setting in *Emma*?

6. *"In **Emma** Jane Austen portrays the life and values of her society with a marvellous fidelity but she does not sufficiently question them."*
   Referring closely to the novel, show whether you agree with this judgement.

Section B:
EMMA'S ERRORS

The structure of the novel reflects her various errors and misunderstandings.

Worksheet 4 – Emma's Errors
The Harriet Smith – Mr Elton affair

1. Norman Sherry in his book *Jane Austen* uses the sub-heading **Emma Self-Deceived** for this first section of the novel:

   a) How does Emma deceive herself about her motives for 'adopting' Harriet Smith? (Ch 3)

   b) What real reasons are implied for this friendship with Harriet?

   c) How do the conversations of Mr Knightley with Mrs Weston (Ch 5) and with Emma herself (Ch 8) shape the reader's attitudes towards the Emma-Harriet relationship?

   List specific page references and brief quotations to support your answers.

2. What errors does Emma's imagination lead her to in her initial judgment of Harriet's background?

3. Trace the **stages** by which Emma manipulates Harriet into refusing Robert Martin's proposal (Ch. 7), thus clearing the way for Mr Elton.

4. *"**How could she have been so deceived ! He protested that he had never thought seriously of Harriet □- never ! She looked back as well as she could, but it was all confusion. She had taken up the idea, she supposed, and made everything bend to it.**"*

   (Emma's thoughts in Ch. 16, after Mr Elton has proposed not to Harriet but to **her**.)
   Look back with Emma at the events leading up to this chapter, using the references below.
   ► What evidence can you find of Emma's making *"everything bend"* to her own idea?
   ► What **clues** are there for the reader that she is misinterpreting Mr Elton's behaviour?
   ► Examples of **irony**?

   References: Ch 6: p 70, p71, p73, pp74-76; Ch 7: p82; Ch 8: pp93-94; Ch 9; Ch 10: pp112-113, pp113-114; Ch 13: pp131-132, p133, pp135-137; Ch 14:pp138-140; Ch 15: pp144-145.

5. **Passage For Close Reading**
   Examine closely the **language** of the passage in which Mr Elton proposes to Emma.
   (Ch. 15 p148 *To restrain him. .. conveyed to Hartfield.* p151.)
   How through both **dialogue** and **description** does Jane Austen convey the emotions of her characters?

6. *"The first error and the worst lay at her door. It was foolish, it was wrong, to take so active a part in bringing any two people together. It was adventuring too far, assuming too much, making light of what ought to be serious, a trick of what ought to be simple. She was quite concerned and ashamed, and resolved to do such things no more."* (Ch. 16 p155)

  a) In what sense has the whole Harriet- Mr Elton affair helped Emma to self- awareness?

  b) Yet how deeply has the lesson penetrated?
    ➢ Examine closely the paragraphs immediately following (to *"getting tolerably out of it."* p156).
    ➢ Has Emma given up matchmaking in later sections of the novel? **evidence? details?**
    (See **Worksheets 5** and **6**.)

7. In this section of the novel Emma does, as Mr Knightley predicts in Ch 8, *"puff (Harriet) up with ... ideas of her own beauty and of what she has a claim to* and does *"raise her expectations too high"*.

    Show how this, ironically, works against Emma in the final section. **references? quotations?**

    In particular find words spoken by Harriet in Chapter 47 which confirm Mr Knightley's prediction.

Essay Questions

7. How does Emma's management of Harriet's affairs reveal the important issues in the novel?

8. *"We see most of the action through Emma's eyes – through a distorting mirror. But she does not know that the mirror distorts."*
    Discuss this proposition, considering especially Jane Austen's treatment of Emma's relationship with Harriet.

9. How is the character of Emma illuminated by being set against other female characters in the novel? Refer in detail to Harriet Smith and at least one other character chosen from: Jane Fairfax, Mrs Elton, Mrs Weston, Miss Bates.

Worksheet 5 – Emma's Errors
The Jane Fairfax – Frank Churchill Episode

Norman Sherry uses the sub-heading **Emma Deceived by Others** for this middle section of the novel, and introduces it with the words *Thus the first act ends. The second begins with the arrival of Jane Fairfax in Highbury, followed by Frank Churchill.*

1. Before considering the deceptions of others, what evidence can you find, despite the good resolutions of Ch 16, that Emma is still the victim of self-deception?
    Find Page References / Quotations to prove that:

    a) she has **not** given up **match-making**, and

    b) her **imagination** is still active.

2. Compare Emma's attitude to Harriet with her attitude to Jane Fairfax:

    a) What is your response to her disagreeable tone at the mention of Jane Fairfax in Chapter 10?

    b) ***Why she did not like Jane Fairfax might be a difficult question to answer*** (Ch 20, p180). What answers can you suggest? Evidence? Page references?

    c) Read closely, in particular, the closing section of Ch 20 (from ***Certain it was that she was to come*** p180 to ***Emma could not forgive her***.) How is our response to Emma influenced by the account of her changing feelings from her first to her second meeting with Jane? Effect of the short sentence with which the chapter closes?

3. Despite her love of match-making, what is Emma's reaction to Mrs Weston's suggestion of a possible match between Jane Fairfax and Mr Knightley? (Ch 26 pp232-237; Ch 33 pp288-290). Evidence of self-deception here? **Irony**? (See also Ch 51 p434)

4. Emma **is** on occasion capable of feeling remorse about her prejudice against Jane Fairfax. Find examples in Ch 33 (p 287) and Ch 34 (p 298).
    (**Who** has prompted this self-examination?)

5. Note the **careful timing** of Frank Churchill's arrival in Highbury just after Jane Fairfax, though earlier he is 'unable' to visit Mrs Weston:

    a) How do Emma and Mr Knightley disagree over the postponement of Frank's visit in Ch 18?

    b) How does Emma's viewpoint contradict what she has said to Mrs Weston in Ch 14? (Reasons**?**)

    c) Whose opinion is later proved correct? (See Frank's letter Ch 50 p424.) (See also, however, Worksheet 7 Q4 (b) and Q4 (c).)

6. *"It is Emma's ironic fate that events should go against her in this way, and that while she is considering Frank as a husband and Jane as crossed in love, she should be made his shield to conceal his intrigue with Jane"* (Norman Sherry)

   a) What **irony** is there in Emma's misreading of Frank's feelings and her own at the end of Chapter 30? By Ch 31 she is no longer *considering Frank as a husband*. How does the last sentence signal more 'errors'?

   b) Using the following references, list all the examples you can find of Frank's deliberately misleading Emma or exploiting her self-deception and *'fancy'*:
   References: Ch 23: pp204-6; Ch 24: pp210-11, pp212-4; Ch 26: pp225-8, p231, p238; Ch 27: pp241-242; Ch 28: pp 248- 249; Ch 29 p260.

   c) What **clues** are we given – to which Emma is blind? What **irony** can you find? (Was this obvious in your first reading or in retrospect? Either way, note Jane Austen's skill.)

"...her error lies in paying so much attention to the young man who went from Weymouth to Ireland that she overlooks the young man who has come from Weymouth to Highbury."
(J F Burrows)

References: Ch 24: p212 (c.f. Ch 25: p216) p213, p214; Ch 26: pp224-5, p234, p235; *Ch 27 pp243-5; Ch 28: p247, p249; Ch 30: p265; Ch 34 pp293ff; Ch 37: p314; Ch 38 p318, pp321-2; Ch 39 p331; *Ch 41: pp341-3, p343ff; Ch 42: pp358-60; Ch 43: p361, p366; *Ch 44: pp373-376.

   d) How is Miss Bates' flow of words often used to give such clues? (See references marked * above)

7. Volume 2 of the original edition ends with the news of Frank Churchill's return to Highbury (Chapters 35, 36). Emma contemplates this at the beginning of Volume 3 (Ch 37). What is **ironic** about her concern for Frank?

8. **A Close Reading Of Chapter 41** (pp 343 ff.)

It is in this chapter that Mr Knightley begins to suspect *some double dealing in Frank's pursuit of Emma* and *a something of private liking, of private understanding even, between Frank Churchill and Jane*. Why?

His suspicions (and jealousy?) are further aroused by the alphabet word game played at Hartfield. (NB: Here the point of view is **not**, as it so often is, Emma's.)

Read this section carefully to find (with the knowledge of hindsight?) answers to the following questions:

> ➤ To what does the word *"blunder"*, offered to Jane Fairfax, refer?
> ➤ Why would the word *"Dixon"*, as Mr Knightley observed, provide **great amusement** to Emma and a **poignant sting** to Jane?
> ➤ Jane Fairfax does not maintain her usual self-control. What different feelings does she reveal during the course of the game?
> ➤ What meaning may have been contained in the letters which Frank **anxiously pushed** towards Jane?[1] Why were they **resolutely swept away... unexamined**?
> ➤ *Frank Churchill comes out of the game very badly. Can he ever seem so charming again after what we see of him here?* (Jennifer Gribble) Do you agree with this judgement of Frank's behaviour in this chapter?
> ➤ Mr Knightley watches the game closely. What is revealed about **him** by his reactions?

Note that at the end of the chapter Emma disagrees with him yet again – *with a confidence which staggered, with a satisfaction which silenced Mr Knightley.*

Essay Questions

10. What uses does Jane Austen make of the role of Jane Fairfax in **Emma**? (NB. *uses* plural).

11. *"One of the advantages, structurally, that are obtained from having a heroine who is deluded is that there is an increase in irony, and the work takes on the interest of the detective story... the reader is given the same clues as the heroine as to what is going on, and he can test his perception against hers"* (Norman Sherry). Discuss the Frank Churchill / Jane Fairfax episode in **Emma** in the light of this comment.

---

1   In the Austens' family tradition it was **pardon** . Other suggestions?

Jane Made Plain: Emma

Worksheet 6 – Emma's Errors:
Humiliation – and Self-Awareness?

1. Volume 3 begins with an over-confident Emma, contemplating Frank Churchill's return. *She did not mean to have her own feelings entangled again, and it would be incumbent on her to avoid any encouragement of his....*

   ... and yet, she could not help rather anticipating something decisive. She felt as if the spring would not pass without bringing a crisis, an event, a something to alter her present composed and tranquil state. (Ch 37 p313). In the light of later events, explain the **ironies** here.

2. In this section Emma's (mis)management of Harriet's affairs and her Frank Churchill 'errors' become entwined.

   a) *Such an adventure as this, – a fine young man and a lovely young woman thrown together in such a way, could hardly fail of suggesting certain ideas to the coldest heart and the steadiest brain. So Emma thought at least. Could a linguist, could a grammarian, could even a mathematician have seen what she did, have witnessed their appearance together, and heard the history of it, without feeling that circumstances had been at work to make them peculiarly interesting to each other? – How much more must an imaginist like herself be on fire with speculation and foresight! – especially with such a ground-work of anticipation as her mind had already made.* (Ch 39 p331)
      - What is the ***adventure*** which has fired Emma's imagination here?
      - What significance is there in the fact that this occurs in the chapter immediately after the ball at the Crown Inn? (See Ch 47 p396-7)
      - Find in Ch31 the ***ground-work*** referred to by Emma.

   b) How accurate is Emma's judgement of Frank and Harriet at this stage of the novel when she confidently asserts, ***He was wishing to get the better of his attachment to herself, she just recovering from her mania for Mr Elton?***

   c) It is particularly **ironic** that Emma's resolution not to be meddling and manipulative as she was in Volume 1 (***Everything was to take its natural course, however, neither impelled nor assisted. She would not stir a step nor drop a hint. No, she had enough of interference. There could be no harm in a scheme, a mere passive scheme. It was no more than a wish. Beyond it she would on no account proceed.*** p332) leads to more complications. Explain this irony, after reading carefully the following sections: Ch 40 especially pp337-9; Ch 47 p393, pp393-400.

3. Before Emma learns the truth about Frank and Harriet she learns an important truth about herself:

   a) Elizabeth Drew says that in her public humiliation of Miss Bates at Box Hill Emma is guilty of the same kind of behaviour as the Eltons at the ball (Ch 38 pp324-5, p327). Are their *later reactions* similar?

   b) Compare the powerful language used for Emma's feelings (end of Ch 43) with her milder self-criticism after the Elton fiasco (Ch 16) and her quick recovery then with now – ***Time did not compose her.*** (See Ch 44.)

   c) How is Mr Knightley important in this episode? (See end of Ch 43, beginning of Ch 44, end of Ch 45.)

> Burrows says of Volume 3: *The earlier part ... is marked by 'social' episodes*[1] *like those that occupy the middle stages of the novel. But, after this brilliant series culminates at Box Hill, Jane Austen suddenly narrows her focus. Most critics write as if the remainder of the novel... which occupies over a hundred pages... amounted only to a proposal and an acceptance. Yet it is here that Jane Austen shows Emma and Mr Knightley patiently resolving their old differences. It is here that she sets most of the earlier action in a new perspective. And it is here, in a final series of quiet but deeply thoughtful conversations that she secures the love between them and shows that it will prosper.*

"From this point ... humiliations fall upon her one after the other. Her world of illusions comes tumbling about her." (Elizabeth Drew)

4. Emma ***jumped with surprise*** at the news of Frank Churchill's secret engagement in Ch 46. Consider in particular the **irony** in her concern for Harriet (Ch 46 p387; Ch 47 p393, p394.)

5. a) What humiliating truth about her influence on Harriet does Emma face in Chapter 47? Ironically, she is still in error. What two past events does she misread? (p400)

    b) What truth about herself does she also acknowledge in this crucial chapter? (pp401-2)

6. Find evidence in Chapter 48 that her self-awareness is still mingled with some self-deception.

7. What comic misunderstanding of motives and emotions occurs in the proposal scene in Chapter 49?

8. What last 'error of imagination' on Emma's part is revealed in the final chapter? (Why does Penny Gay, pointing out that Emma has cast Harriet as the heroine of a romance, speak of the novel as *Austen's anti-romance?*)

9. A review of Emma's errors. Norman Page's reading:
    > *One of the features of Jane Austen's method is to give variety within the process of repetition, so that although Emma makes a number of mistakes the underlying elements are often different. The mistake over Mr Elton is a case of simple misinterpretation: he makes no attempt to mislead – indeed to anyone but the over-confident Emma and the easily-led Harriet his behaviour would have been unambiguous, and Mr Knightley at least guesses the truth. When it comes to the errors over Jane Fairfax and Frank Churchill, the situation is different, in that actual dissimulation is involved: these two are playing a game of deliberate deceit, and Emma is not the only one to be hoodwinked (though again Mr Knightley has an inkling of the truth). Another minor error, Emma's short-lived belief that Frank is in love with her, is encouraged by Frank's behaviour, which is again deliberately deceptive. Finally, the knowledge of Mr Knightley's true feelings, and of her own heart, are only arrived at after a more profound kind of self-deception has been thrown off. The tone of these episodes progressively deepens, from the light comedy of Mr Elton's synthetic gallantry and eventual mortification, to the sombre depression of Emma's belief (one more error, as it turns out) that she has ruined her own chances of happiness by bringing Harriet and Mr Knightly together, forcing from her the passionate exclamation **Oh God! that I had never seen her!***

---

1   See Worksheet 3: Group Work topics 4, 5 and 6.

What lessons has Emma learned? How much has she changed by the end of the novel?

10. Emma's self-reproaches (Chapter 47: p398 and p402) are presented in very strong language but it is the idea that Mr Knightley loves Harriet that produces the words **evil** (twice), **debasement, horrible, dreadful**, and makes her cry out against the world as full of things **unequal, inconsistent, incongruous**. Vivien Jones sees this as *what is perhaps the final irony*, that she is only aware of her faults because she is now aware of her feelings, and raises the question *whether Emma would have seen her own selfishness if she hadn't been in love with Mr Knightley*. What do you think?

11. Is there real self-knowledge in the following sections of Chapter 48? (before Mr Knightley's return):
    - her regrets about Miss Bates (p404) and Jane Fairfax (p409);
    - the resolutions for the future with which the chapter concludes.

12. Comment on the tone of the conversation with Mr Knightley about Harriet (Chapter 54 pp452-6) – especially Emma's words in response to his claim that she has changed: *I hope so – for at that time I was a fool* – and her later reflections (pp456-7)

13. By the end of the novel Emma has lost **the disposition to think a little too well of herself** and her self-deception. Has she also lost her lively, assertive spirit? Consider the following readings:

    - Vivien Jones:
      Is the cost of her learning to deserve her social position too great? To what extent has she given up her independence of mind, however mistaken it sometimes proved to be?

    - Sandra Gilbert and Susan Gubar[1]:
      Austen's story is especially flattering to male readers because it describes the taming of not just any woman but . . . of a rebellious, imaginative woman who is amorously mastered by a sensible man.

    - Julia Prewitt Brown:
      Emma's personality opens like a fan before us. Seen in her innumerable relationships with others, she alters continually and gracefully, and the novel is deliberately paced to allow this. Mr Woodhouse's daughter is not Harriet's patroness or Mr John Knightley's sister-in-law. The Emma who condescends to Harriet, self-satisfied, smirking and dictatorial, is not the Emma we see with Mr Knightley, witty, open and daring. And although she is tied by countless social relations, she is neither overshadowed nor borne down by them. Emma's inner nature, her stability as Emma, even as she is drawn this way and that – spoiled, criticised, disappointed, insulted, and loved – never alters; She is still Emma.

---

1   These critics say authorship for Austen is an escape from the very restraints she imposes on her female characters. She can create Mary Crawford's witty letters (in *Mansfield Park*) or Emma's brilliant retorts even while rejecting them as improper.

12. *"Emma's faults constantly threaten to produce serious harm."* With this idea in mind, examine how Jane Austen achieves a predominantly comic tone in the novel.

13. *"Mr Knightley consistently sees the true nature of things; Emma is concerned only with their appearance."*
To what extent does this comment apply to each character in your reading of the novel?

14. Using the importance of this extract as a starting point, examine the way Jane Austen presents Emma's character and the ironic techniques used in the novel as a whole.
"There does seem to be a something in the air of Hartfield which gives love exactly the right direction and sends it into the very channel where it ought to flow.
The course of true love never did run smooth –
A Hartfield edition of Shakespeare would have a long note on that passage." (Emma to Harriet in Chapter 9)

15. *"Snobbery, smugness, condescension, thoughtlessness, unkindness, vanity, selfishness and self-deception – all these human failings are criticised by Jane Austen"*
Is Emma the only character who shows such faults?

16. **Till now that she was threatened with its loss, Emma had never known how much of her happiness depended on being first with Mr Knightley, first in interest and affection.** (Ch 48). How has Jane Austen prepared the reader throughout the novel for this discovery which Emma makes so belatedly?

17. **"Seldom, very seldom does complete truth belong to any human disclosure; seldom can it happen that something is not a little disguised or a little mistaken"**. (Ch 49 – immediately after Emma's acceptance of Mr Knightley's proposal.)
 ➤ Discuss this comment in the light of the comic irony of the events that have led up to it.
 ➤ How does it also relate to Jane Austen's serious concerns in the novel?

18. Discuss the proposition that
"in most of the book Jane Austen's satire and irony are directed as much at Emma as at Mrs Elton. – What Mrs Elton does in a vulgar, loud way, Emma does in a more refined and ladylike way ."

19. Jane Austen called Emma *"a heroine whom no-one but myself will much like"* but many readers like Emma. Discuss the methods used by Austen to create a sympathetic response to Emma despite her faults.

20. **"Emma** *is a novel about self-deception but it is also about self discovery"*
Do you agree?

Section C:
MAINLY
MALES

═══════════
═══════════
═══════════

Worksheet 7
The Men in Emma's Life

1. Mr Woodhouse

I believe few married women are half as much mistress of their husband's house as I am of Hartfield; and never, never could I expect to be so truly beloved and important; so always first and always right in any man's eyes as I am in my father's.
(Ch 10: Emma confidently claiming to Harriet that she will never marry.)

a) How does this contribute to what Austen calls in Ch 1 **the real evils** of Emma's situation?

b) Despite her faults, is Emma's patience with her father one of her redeeming qualities? (details? evidence?)

2. Mr Elton

What is Mr Elton's attitude to Emma: a) before and b) after the scene in the carriage in Chapter 15?

References: a) Chapters 6, 7, 9, 10, 13, 14, 15. b) Chapters 15, 17, 21, 22, 32, 38.

3. Frank Churchill

a) Emma's first meeting with the much talked about Frank Churchill comes in Chapter 23. Explain the irony of this chapter's containing both the **suspicion of what might be expected of their knowing each other, which had taken strong possession of her mind** and the beginning of Frank's duplicity. (See Worksheet 5 – Q 6, 7, 8.)

b) Emma prides herself on her self-awareness as she examines her feelings for Frank in Chapter 31 – **irony**? How is her ignorance of her own emotional state suggested in Ch 38 (See Q4 d below) and confirmed in Ch 47?

c) When Emma learns the truth about Frank in Chapter 46 she says **So unlike what a man should be! – None of that upright integrity, that strict adherence to truth and principle, that disdain of trick and littleness, which a man should display in every transaction of his life.**
What man might she be thinking of who does have these qualities?

4. Mr Knightley

a) Emma's relationship with Mr Knightley is established in Chapter 1 when his visit rescues her from a cheerless evening with her father. What have we learned by the end of the chapter? Quotations to illustrate?

b) i) Christopher Gillie says *From the beginning he has represented honest, disinterested insight and concern.* **Is** Mr Knightley always disinterested? Consider what we are told in Chapter 49 (p419) **On his side there had been a long-standing jealousy, old as the arrival, or even the expectation, of Frank Churchill.** Re-read the conversation between Mr Knightley and Emma in Ch 18. What signs can you find of his jealousy?

   ii) How do the following sections of the novel also hint at or suggest such feelings?
   - Ch 28 his change of mind in response to Miss Bates's invitation.
   - Ch 30 his attitude to the planned ball.
   - Ch 33 his reaction to the idea that he is interested in Jane Fairfax.
   - Ch 38 his *grave* looks and *often observing* her as Emma dances.
   - Ch 41 his concern after the alphabet game and his mood as he leaves.
   - Ch 45 his sudden trip to London after the picnic at Box Hill.

c) Read carefully the retrospective account of Mr Knightley's actions, motives and feelings in Ch 49 pp 419-20. Note the mingling of Knightley's point-of-view and the narrator's voice. What is the tone of the final paragraph?

d) The ball at the Crown Inn (Ch 38) is an important stage in the relationship of Emma and Mr Knightley. Consider:

   i) Emma's thoughts as she watches him (from ***She was more disturbed by Mr Knightley's not dancing***). Can you find evidence that she is (unconsciously) attracted to him?

   ii) Julia Prewitt Brown's reading:

The scene at the Crown Ball when Mr Knightley asks the defenceless and snubbed Harriet to dance is alive with the sense of a new understanding between Emma and Mr Knightley. Until the end of the chapter no words are spoken between them. – Eye contact replaces speech: **her countenance said much, as soon as she could catch his eye again.** *And the wonderfully powerful:* **her eyes invited him to come to her and be thanked.** *One feels that this is what being in love is about, not all the talk, planning, and invention Emma imagines it is.*
It is the power to move, to know the other person.

The Crown Ball is a scene of extraordinary delicacy and love. ... its strength lies in Emma's watching Mr Knightley perform this act of kindness; her appreciation of it makes her a better Emma than the Emma who mistreats the Martins, the Emma who is above everyone. And Mr Knightley, who would do what he does now for any woman in the novel, does it here for Emma, as they both know. . . . The scene ends in dance:

"Will you?" said he, offering his hand.
"Indeed I will. You have shown that you can dance, and you know we are not really so much brother and sister as to make it at all improper."
"Brother and sister! no, indeed."

Mr Knightley knows he loves Emma at this point; characteristically Emma does not yet know she loves him. But the reader is not ignorant and this knowledge gives the scene its exquisite emotion.

e) Most critics admire Mr Knightley, seeing him as exemplifying what is highest in Jane Austen's scale of values.

   ▶ *More than any other male character in Jane Austen's novels, Mr Knightley seems to stand for an ideal in her conception of a civilised man of the class to which she belonged: practical but with deep feeling, robust but delicate in perception, energetically direct but with deep powers of restraint; above all, strongly traditional in his sense of what is owing to the obligations of his status and to people.* (Christopher Gillie)

   ▶ The reading of J F Burrows is slightly different: arguing that George Knightley is fallible and imperfect in his way, just as Emma is in hers, he draws attention to the words at the end of Chapter 49 after the proposal scene – ***This one half hour had given to each the same precious certainty of being beloved, had cleared from each the same degree of ignorance, jealousy or distrust.***

Whichever is your reading, is the following true?
In relation to the other male characters of the novel, he is clearly a superior being in integrity, intelligence and consideration for others.

See also Essay Questions 13 and 16.

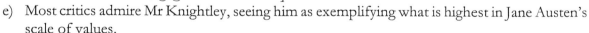

Section D:
"EMMA" AS A
COMIC NOVEL

Worksheet 8
The Definition of Comedy

Underline sections of the following extracts (from critical essays on *Emma*) which throw light on the term **comedy**.

From *Jane Austen: A Lecture* by A C Bradley

But Jane Austen's attitude, we may even say her instinctive attitude, is, of course, that of the humorist. And this is not all. The foibles, illusions, self-contradictions, of human nature are a joy to her for their own sakes, but also because through action they lead to consequences which may be serious but may also be comic. In that case they sometimes produce matter fit for a comedy, a play in which people's lives fall into an entanglement of errors, cross-purposes, and misunderstandings, from which they are rescued, not by their own wisdom or skill, but by the kindness of Fortune or some Providence with a weakness for lovers . . .

But the resemblance to comedy goes further: it extends to the whole story. In all her novels, though in varying degrees, Jane Austen regards the characters, good and bad alike, with ironical amusement, because they never see the situation as it really is and as she sees it. This is the deeper source of our unbroken pleasure in reading her. We constantly share her point of view, and are aware of the amusing difference of the fact and its appearance to the actors. If you fail to perceive and enjoy this you are not reading Jane Austen. Some readers do not perceive it, and therefore fail to appreciate her. Others perceive it without enjoying it, and they think her cynical. She is never cynical, and not often merely satirical. A cynic or mere satirist may be intellectually pleased by human absurdities and illusions, but he does not feel them to be good. But to Jane Austen, so far as they are not seriously harmful, they are altogether pleasant, because they are both ridiculous and right. It is amusing, for example, that Knightley, who is almost a model of good sense, right feeling and just action, should be unjust to Frank Churchill because, though he does not know it, he himself is in love with Emma: but to Jane Austen that is not only the way a man is made but the way he should be made. No doubt there are plenty of things that should not be, but when we so regard them they are not comical. A main point of difference between Jane Austen and Johnson is that to her much more of the world is amusing, and much more of it is right. She is less of a moralist and more of a humorist . . .

Most of the characters are involved in the contrast of reality and illusion, but it is concentrated on Emma. This young lady, who is always surpassingly confident of being right, is always surpassingly wrong. She is reputed very clever, and she is clever, and she never sees the fact and never understands herself. A spoiled child, with a good disposition and more will than most of the people in her little world, she begins to put this world to rights. She chooses for a friend, not Jane Fairfax, her equal, but the amiable, soft, stupid and adoring Harriet Smith. Her motive, which she supposes to be kindness, is the pleasure of patronage and management. She detaches Harriet's affections from a suitable lover, and fastens them on a person wholly unsuitable and perfectly indifferent. Convinced that she has won Mr Elton for Harriet, she finds that, in fact, her operations have encouraged him to aspire to herself. Leaving Harriet, on the explosion of this bubble, to recover from her disappointment, she next chooses to fancy that she herself and Frank

Churchill, who is coming to visit his father, are likely to fall in love; while, in fact, he is coming solely because is secretly engaged to Jane Fairfax. Without any reason she supposes Jane to be enamoured of somebody else's husband and imparts her suspicion, of all people, to Jane's lover. Having discovered that her own love for him was fictitious, she now encourages Harriet Smith to fall in love with him; but as she omits to mention his name, she succeeds without knowing it, in attaching Harriet to Mr Knightley instead. In her satisfaction at finding herself out of love with Frank Churchill, and observing none of those signs of his relation to Jane Fairfax which are obvious to Mr Knightley, she flirts outrageously with him, involves Jane in misery, and only escapes by accident from ruining the happiness of the pair. Finally, discovering to her dismay that she has led Harriet to raise her eyes to Knightley, and to raise them, in Harriet's opinion, not in vain, she also discovers, to her still greater dismay, that she loves Knightley herself, and then, to her delight, that she is beloved by him. She has reached a fact at last, but only by the benevolence of Fortune, who crowns her kindness by taking the heart of Harriet and flinging it, like a piece of putty, at her original lover. In a sketch like this the comedy of the story loses both its fun and its verisimilitude, but we know how delightful it is, and on the whole how true to nature.

From an article in *The Quarterly Review* July 1917 by Reginald Farrar

For this is the novel of character, and of character alone, and of one dominating character in particular. And many a rash reader, and some who are not rash, have been shut out on the threshold of Emma's Comedy by a dislike of Emma herself. Well did Jane Austen know what she was about when she said, **"I am going to take a heroine whom nobody but myself will much like"**. No one who carefully reads the three opening paragraphs of the book can entertain a doubt . . . for in these the author gives us quite clear warning of what we are to see. We are to see the gradual humiliation of self-conceit, through a long self-wrought succession of disasters, serious in effect, but keyed in Comedy throughout. Emma herself, in fact, is never to be taken seriously. And it is only those who have not realised this who will be 'put off' by her absurdities, her snobberies, her misdirected mischievous ingenuities. Emma is simply a figure of fun. To conciliate affection for a character not because of its charms, but in defiance of its defects is the loftiest aim of the comic spirit; Shakespeare achieved it with his besotted old rogue of a Falstaff, and Molière with Celimène [1]. It is with these, not with 'sympathetic' heroines, that Emma takes rank, as the culminating figure of English high-comedy. And to attain success in creating a being whom you both love and laugh at, the author must attempt a task of complicated difficulty. He must run with the hare and hunt with the hounds, treat his creation at once objectively and subjectively, get inside it to inspire it with sympathy, and yet stay outside it to direct laughter at its comic aspects. And this is what Jane Austen does for Emma, with a consistent sublimity so demure that indeed a reader accustomed only to crude work might be pardoned for missing the point of her innumerable hints, and actually taking seriously, for example, the irony with which Emma's attitude about the Coles' dinner-party is treated, or the even more convulsive comedy of Emma's reflections after it. But only Jane Austen is capable of such oblique glints of humour; and only in Emma does she weave them so densely into her kaleidoscope that the reader must be perpetually on his guard lest some specially delicious flash escape his notice or some touch of dialogue be taken for the author's own intention . . . Yet, as Emma really does behave extremely ill by Jane Fairfax, and even worse by Robert Martin, merely to laugh would not be enough, and every disapproval would justly be deepened to dislike. But, when we realise that each machination of Emma's, each imagined piece of penetration, is to be a thread in the snare woven

1   Characters in *King Henry IV* (Falstaff = a gluttonous drunkard) and *The Misanthrope* (Celimène = a flirt)

unconsciously by herself for her own enmeshing in disaster, then the balance is rectified again, and disapproval can lighten to laughter once more. . . . we are kept so dancing up and down with alternate rage and delight at Emma that finally, when we see her self-esteem hammered bit by bit into collapse the nemesis would be too severe were she to be left in the depths. By the merciful intention of the book, however, she is saved in the very nick of time, by what seems like a happy accident, but is really the outcome of her own unsuspected good qualities, just as much as her disasters had been the outcome of her own most cherished follies.

Now write your own definition of comedy in literature.

Worksheet 9
The Comic Characters

1. *"Mrs Elton, Miss Bates and Mr Woodhouse are essentially caricatures, with fixed mannerisms and a limited number of qualities, on which they depend for the comic effect they produce."* (Frank Bradbrook)

   For each of the characters named above list briefly:

   a) the mannerisms or qualities of character which distinguish them and make them amusing;

   b) one or two episodes or incidents in which these qualities are revealed. Page references?

2. An important element in Austen's comic characterisation is **the way these characters speak.**

   a) **Miss Bates**

   Find examples of Miss Bates' dialogue and analyse what makes it comic. Page references? Note however the importance of this seemingly silly dialogue to the plot (see Worksheet 5) and the dignity of her reaction when Emma ridicules her at Box Hill.

   b) **Mrs Elton**

   i)   In Mrs Elton's dialogue certain topics or phrases recur frequently. Can you identify these? (What makes her conversation with Mr Weston in Chapter 36 so funny?)

   ii) **Passage For Close Reading:**
        Examine closely the following extract from the account of the strawberry party at Donwell Abbey Ch 42 p353 (from ***The whole party was assembled*** to p354 ***How Jane could bear it at all, was astonishing to Emma.***) How is the language and style used to reveal Mrs Elton's character?
        NB: Comment in particular on the word choice in *was in raptures* and *was wild to have the offer closed.*

   iii) Mrs Elton's voice is heard again in the novel's concluding paragraph. (p465)
        Comment on the effect created by this final example of her dialogue.

   c) **Mr Woodhouse**

   i)   Add to the following examples of Mr Woodhouse's dialogue further quotations selected to illustrate the character trait revealed here.

   - ➤ *"An egg boiled soft is not unwholesome. Searle understands boiling an egg better than anybody. I would not recommend an egg boiled by any body else."*

   - ➤ *"Do not tell his father but that young man is not quite the thing. He has been opening the doors very often this evening, and keeping them open very inconsiderately. He does not think of the draught. I do not mean to set you against him, but indeed he is not quite the thing!"*

Examine closely the conversation between Mr Woodhouse and Isabella in Ch 12 (from p123 *"My poor dear Isabella* . . . to p128 *as he could himself"* Comment on Jane Austen's word choice in the sentence in which she introduces this conversation: *enjoying a full flow of <u>happy regrets</u> and <u>fearful affection</u> with his daughter* and analyse the way the language and style of the whole passage reveals the characters of Mr Woodhouse, of Isabella and of her husband. Emma says comparatively little. How does her role contribute to the humour?

Chapter 34 (Mr Woodhouse):
I am very sorry to hear Miss Fairfax, of your being out this morning in the rain.

Worksheet 10
Comedy Continued

1. Irony Used For Comic Effect

a) Consider how often Jane Austen's **irony** is the source of comedy in the novel (on first reading or in retrospect) **and** how often this is directed at Emma herself.
   Find sections in which the reader derives amusement from being 'in the know' while Emma is (smugly) ignorant.

b) Elizabeth Drew claims that Jane Austen uses a series of scenes of ironic parallel and contrasts to show how much Emma has in common with the character she dislikes so much, Mrs Elton.
   The first time she meets Mrs Elton she sums her up in words which might almost be an unkind description of herself.

   i) Find these words in Chapter 32 (actually the second meeting **When the visit was returned . . .**)

   ii) *What Mrs Elton does in a vulgar, loud way, Emma does in a more refined and ladylike way*
      How many examples can you find to support this reading?

   (See also **Worksheet 11, Austen's Irony**)

2. The Comic Resolution- or -Happy Ending

> One definition of Comedy is that all misunderstandings, difficulties, or plot complications are resolved or sorted out in a happy ending. This is called the comic resolution or dénouement (French dénouer = to disentangle or unknot)

a) *"comedy . . . is a play in which a situation holds some threat of disaster but issues in the achievement of happiness; and those comedies may satisfy us most deeply when danger is averted and the happiness achieved through something that takes place in the characters."* (Harold Jenkins on Shakespeare's *Twelfth Night*) Consider how well this applies to Austen's novel:

   i) To what extent can the happy ending be said to be achieved by *"something that takes place in"* Emma?

   ii) What *disaster* has threatened Jane Fairfax? What (rather convenient?) plot device brings her *happiness*?

iii) How does Harriet contribute to a 'happy ending' in which the *threat of disaster* is averted?

➤ Is her behaviour here consistent with Jane Austen's characterisation of her throughout the novel?
(See Bradley's comment on *the benevolence of Fortune* quoted in **Worksheet 8**, The **Definition of Comedy**.)

➤ Has Mr Knightley (as well as 'Fortune') played a role in her reconciliation with Robert Martin?

➤ Read the paragraph in Chapter 54 (from *serious she was* to *such a Harriet!*) Though these are Emma's reflections might we also interpret *She must laugh at such a close!* as Austen's smiling acknowledgement of the artificiality of this comic resolution?

b) The opening of the novel has presented Mr Woodhouse's dislike of marriage as humorous[1] but at the end this appears to be a serious obstacle to Emma's happiness. (Penny Gay says *"he seems to have forgotten the facts of life".*)

How does his motivation for consenting to the wedding of his daughter and Mr Knightley add to the comedy and undermine the sentimentality of the 'happy ending'?
(Is Mrs Elton used in the same way in the novel's final paragraph?)

Essay Questions linked to Worksheets 8, 9 and 10

21. *"The real evils, indeed, of Emma's situation were the power the power of having rather too much her own way, and a disposition to think a little too well of herself."* How does Jane Austen use these "evils" for comic effect in her novel?

22. *"Mr Woodhouse, so wrongly and oddly regarded as an old pet by generations of readers, is actually a menace."* (Ronald Blythe)
Do you agree? Discuss Jane Austen's characterisation of Mr Woodhouse and his role in the novel.

23. *"Follies and nonsense, whims and inconsistencies do divert me and I laugh at them whenever I can."*
The above are the words of a character in another of Austen's novels, **Pride and Prejudice**. How does Jane Austen reveal such a response to the world in **Emma**?

24. *"What incomparable noodles she exhibits for our astonishment and laughter!"*
(G H Lewes in 1859) Which **two** comic characters in *Emma* do you think most arouse astonishment and laughter? Why?

25. *Even when Emma acknowledges her love for Mr Knightley, there are comic misunderstandings and Jane Austen ironically undercuts the sentimentality of the conventional 'happy ending' with comedy.*
Examine the concluding section of the novel in the light of this reading.

26. *"In Jane Austen's novels we find a serious criticism of life expressed in terms of comedy"*
Discuss this proposition with reference to **Emma**.

See also essay questions 12, 14, 15, 17 and 18 on previous Worksheets.

---

1 See comments on *"poor Miss Taylor"* (Ch 1) and attitude to wedding cake (end Ch 2).

Section E:
AUSTEN'S IRONY

Worksheet 11
A Review of Austen's Use of Irony

Consider how often the word **irony** or **ironic** appears in the previous Worksheets (including the Essay Questions). This highlights the importance of Jane Austen's use of irony as a comic technique in her novel.

The Concept of Irony

➤ The two principal kinds of irony might be classified as **Verbal Irony** and **Situational Irony**.

➤ The common element of all irony is a difference between appearance and reality. An ironist seems to be saying one thing but is really saying something quite different (ie, presents an appearance and pretends to be unaware of the reality); a victim of irony is confident that things are what they seem and unaware that they are really quite different (ie, is deceived by an appearance and unaware of the reality).

➤ Throughout this novel a major source of the comic effect is in the discrepancy between what Emma **thinks** is true (and her smugness in this knowledge) and what in fact **is** true. Sometimes the irony may be detected on a first reading; sometimes it is very obvious only with hindsight.

Examples From The Novel

A few examples of different types are given to get you started. Add to the list giving page/chapter references.

1. **Verbal Irony** (in *Austen's choice of language*)

   ➤ description of Harriet's silly collection of riddles as a ***literary pursuit*** (Chapter 9).

   ➤ dinner conversation (Ch 26): ***nothing worse than every day remarks, dull repetitions, old news and heavy jokes.***

2. **Situational Irony –**

   i) (*the victim unaware but strong clues to 'the truth' for the reader*)

   ➢ Emma's thoughts on Mr Elton's charade (Ch 9)
   Humph – Harriet's ready wit! All the better. A man must be very much in love to describe her so. Ah! Mr Knightley, I wish you had the benefit of this; I think this would convince you. For once in your life you would be obliged to own yourself mistaken.

> Emma's judgement of her brother-in-law (Ch 13)
> *the blunders which often arise from a partial knowledge of circumstance ..,*
> *the mistakes which people of high pretensions to judgment are for ever*
> *falling into*

ii) (*obvious in retrospect -- a strong contrast between 'the truth' and the victim's unawareness*)

> many details of conversations between Emma and Frank Churchill about Jane
> Fairfax / Mr Dixon / the piano – eg, Chapter 26 *"And now I can see it in no*
> *other light but as an offering of love"* Chapter 28?

> Emma's belief that she is being cautious in instructing Harriet *"Let no name ever*
> *pass our lips"*. (Ch 40)

3. **Ironic Parallels And Contrasts** (Emma and Mrs Elton)

➤ Emma's attitude to the Coles (Ch 25) and Mrs Elton's to the Tupman family of
Birmingham (Ch 36)

➤ *extremely well satisfied with herself and thinking much of her own importance*
(Emma's judgement of Mrs Elton Ch 32).

Suggestions For Further Reading And Viewing

Reading

The following critical works are referred to in this order in the worksheets:

Elizabeth Drew   *The Novel:: A Modern Guide To Fifteen English Masterpieces* Dell 1963.

Ronald Blythe   Introduction and Notes to Penguin English Library edition *Emma* 1966.

Penny Gay   *Jane Austen's "Emma"* Horizon Studies in Literature, Sydney University Press 1995.

Arnold Kettle   *"Emma"* in *An Introduction To The English Novel Part 111* Arrow 1951. (reprinted in *Jane Austen: A Collection Of Critical Essays* ed Ian Watt).

Frank W Bradbrook   *Jane Austen: "Emma"* Edward Arnold 1961.

Oliver MacDonagh   *Jane Austen – Real and Imagined Worlds* Routledge 1998.

A Walton Litz   from *Jane Austen: A Study of Her Artistic Development* *

Christopher Gillie   *A Preface To Jane Austen* Longman 1974.

Sandra M Gilbert & Susan Gubar   *Jane Austen's Cover Story* (in *The Madwoman In The Attic: The Woman Writer and the Nineteenth Century Literary Imagination*) Yale University Press 1979.

Norman Sherry   *Jane Austen* Evans Brothers 1966.

J F Burrows   *Jane Austen's "Emma"* Sydney University Press (Methuen) 1969.

Jennifer Gribble   *Meaning in "Emma"* (in *Perspectives 78* ed Fox and McFarlane Sorrett 1978).

Norman Page   *"Emma" by Jane Austen* Macmillan 1985.

Vivien Jones   *Judgment and Irony: "Emma"* (in *How To Study A Jane Austen Novel* Macmillan 1987).

Julia Prewitt Brown   *Jane Austen's Novels* Harvard University Press 1979.

A C Bradley   from *Jane Austen: A Lecture* *

Reginald Farrar   from the *Quarterly Review* CCXXVIII (July 1917)*

* (reprinted in Norton Critical Edition ed Stephen M Parrish, W W Norton & Co 1972).

Other Recommended Works

David Lodge ed.   *Jane Austen's "Emma": A Selection Of Critical Essays* Macmillan (Casebook)1968

Claudia L Johnson   *Jane Austen: Women, Politics and the Novel* University of Chicago Press 1988

Wayne Booth   *Control Of Distance in Jane Austen's "Emma"* (in the Norton Critical Edition)

Mark Schorer   *The Humiliation of Emma Woodhouse* (in *Jane Austen A Collection Of Critical Essays* ed. Ian Watt Prentice-Hall 1963)

Andrew H. Wright   *Jane Austen's Novels: A Study In Structure* Chatto & Windus 1961.

Yasmine Gooneratne   *Jane Austen* Cambridge University Press 1970

Mary Lascelles   *Jane Austen And Her Art* Oxford University Press 1939

Norman Page   *The Language Of Jane Austen* Basil Blackwell 1972

Viewing

1. **BBC TV SERIES** directed by John Glenister 1993 with Doran Godwin as Emma and John Carson as Mr Knightley. Available at ABC Shops and on Video.

2. **FILM** written by Andrew Davies and directed by Diarmuid Lawrence 1996 with Kate Beckinsale as Emma and Mark Strong as Mr Knightley. A United Film and Television production of Meridian Broadcasting. Available on video. (See *The Making Of Jane Austen's Emma* S Birtwhistle & S Conklin Penguin 1996).

3. **FILM** written for the screen and directed by Douglas Mcgrath 1996 with Gwyneth Paltrow as Emma and Jeremy Northam as Mr Knightley. Available on video.

4. **FILM** *Clueless* written and directed by Amy Heckerling 1995 starring Alicia Silverstone as Cher (Emma). Available on video.

1. BBC TV Series

➤ Obviously the BBC TV Series, screened as 6 one-hour episodes, is longer and more detailed, including more of Jane Austen's dialogue such as Frank Churchill's disparaging comments on Jane Fairfax's hairstyle (Ch 26) or the fuss about Jane's visit to the Post Office (Ch 34). Are such seemingly small details important?

➤ It deals with almost all the **Social Occasions** on **Worksheet 1** in detail (but combines the last two — the Donwell strawberry picking and the Box Hill picnic — rather than having them take place on consecutive days. Effect?)

2. FILM starring Kate Beckinsale

➤ This film uses much of Austen's dialogue and faithfully presents a number of key episodes in the novel. All six social occasions are included, though not all in the same detail as in the novel. (Frank's blunder and the alphabet word game from Ch 41 are incorporated into the later Box Hill episode of Ch 43.)

➤ Some of the ways in which the novel's ideas are translated into the medium of film.

close-ups and point-of-view shots:
➢ hopes of Mr and Mrs Weston for Emma / Frank suggested by significant looks
➢ Emma's face as she misreads Frank's beginning of a confession
➢ shot of Harriet and Mr Knightley together in the lime walk at Donwell (watched by Emma)
➢ Emma's reaction to Mr Knightley's reproof at Box Hill.
Other examples?

use of the camera to suggest 'clues' about the Frank Churchill/Jane Fairfax relationship:
➢ Frank's talk near Mr Elton's home of sharing a small house *with the woman you love*;
➢ cutting from discussion of Frank's visit to London to sound effect of piano music + shot of piano being hauled through Miss Bates's window;
➢ shot of Frank and Jane moving apart ; Frank and Jane often in same shot though only one in close focus e.g. dinner party scene: Frank near Emma agreeing that piano is an *offering of love* – Jane in same shot .
Other examples?

fantasy sequences to suggest Emma's qualities as *an imaginist*
- ➤ Harriet/Mr Elton wedding
- ➤ Frank Churchill's portrait speaking to Emma
- ➤ Jane/Mr Knightley wedding – Emma in the church crying *No!*
- ➤ Harriet/Mr Knightley wedding– repeat of Emma crying *No!* scene

Other examples?

**use of flashbacks to suggest Emma's final self-knowledge
and the irony obvious in a second reading**
- ➤ Mrs Weston's words *It was he who sent the piano* ⇢ flashback to Jane at the piano and Frank singing + repeat of Frank's voice *It was a gift of love*
- ➤ Emma's words *Oh God that I had never seen her!* ⇢ flashback of Emma and Mr Knightley dancing, mingled with Harriet/Knightley wedding fantasy, flashback of reconciliation scene with Isabella's baby, repeat of dancing flashback + Mr Knightley's voice *Brother and sister, no indeed!*

**Visual representation of the weather moods used by
Austen to back Emma's emotions (Chapters 48 and 49)**
- ➤ shot of heavy grey clouds moving across sky
- ➤ the garden after rain as setting for proposal scene

- ► Additions/alterations?
  - ➤ The most obvious is the way the film shows not only the comfortable lives of Austen's gentry but the servants, the agricultural labourers, the poor, the gypsies. For example, servants placing cushions for Mrs Elton to kneel on at the strawberry party or toiling up the slope of Box Hill with picnic gear.
  - ➤ effect of adding the poultry-thieves to the opening as well as the conclusion?
  - ➤ effect of the following invented scenes and speeches?
    - i) **Emma** (looking down on view of Donwell) *All this is Mr Knightley's* **Harriet** *The sparrows and the skylarks don't belong to Mr Knightley, do they?* **Emma** *Perhaps not but the woodcocks and the pheasants do.*
    - ii) celebration of the coming marriage in a 'harvest festival' scene – *Mr Knightley's* 'good landowner' speech *By this time next year I will be living at Hartfield, though I assure you all I shall still be farming my estate . . . There will be stability, there will be continuation.*
    - iii) reversal of the dialogue from the earlier ball scene in this conclusion: **Mr Knightley** *Will you dance with me, Emma? You and I are not so much brother and sister as to make it improper.* **Emma** *Brother and sister, no indeed!*

- ► The conclusion: effect of
  - ➤ the camera's focusing on the three couples who join the set to lead the dancing? – then moving outside as poultry thieves strike?
  - ➤ mingled sound effects of music from the dancing and cackling fowls and the final shot of the moon?

- ► Casting:

The age difference between Emma and Mr Knightley is retained. Is this important? (Compare Film 3.)

3. FILM Starring Gwyneth Paltrow

➤ This film, advertised with the words *This summer Cupid is armed and dangerous !*, casts with Gwyneth Paltrow's young and pretty Emma a handsome (and young?) Jeremy Northam as Mr Knightley. How, well does this express the main concerns of the novel which Penny Gay calls *Austen's anti-romance*?

➤ Patricia Rozema, director of *Mansfield Park*, responded to an interviewer's comment that the whole film is *a little too sweet* with *A little! like put some more syrup on your candy!* Rozema says she began the draft of her film with *This aint no garden party* . Compare the 'chocolate-box' atmosphere created by McGrath — especially the actual garden settings (the tent/the archery scene/Harriet's butterfly net among the blossoms).

➤ The Donwell Abbey outing is omitted from the Social Occasions (though the characters appear to be picking strawberries on the side of Box Hill). Importance of this outing in Austen? (See Worksheet 3 Groups 5 & 6)

➤ How well is Austen's irony (both the narrator's voice and irony of situation) translated to the medium of film?
Consider the use of Mrs Weston's voice-over in the introduction and conclusion **and** Emma's voiced thoughts, for example when Jane Fairfax evades questions about Frank or - in response to Harriet's *Goodbye Mr Elton* as she destroys her 'treasures' – *Hello, Mr Churchill!*
Is the viewer given the 'clues' about the Frank/Jane relationship which a reader can find in the novel?

➤ Effect of additions/alterations. For example:
  ➢ the first meeting of Frank and Emma?
  ➢ the Mr Dixon idea being suggested by Frank rather than Emma?
A silly scene of Harriet's ineptness in the visit to the poor cottagers is invented, but Austen's comic use of the poultry-thieves is omitted from the ending (though the intrusion of Mrs Elton into the novel's final paragraph is well captured by her speaking directly to the camera in the concluding wedding scene.)

➤ Some of the invented dialogue invites comparison with Jane Austen's language. For example:
  ➢ Emma on Mrs Elton *Is it possible that Mr Elton met her while doing charity work in a mental infirmary?*
  ➢ the proposal scene **Emma** *Oh, dear !* **Mr Knightley** *What?* **Emma** *Oh, something about the deer we need for the venison stew.*
  ➢ **Mr Knightley** *Marry me, my wonderful, darling friend?*

If time permits the viewing of more than one of the above versions this could lead to **comparisons** such as

Particular Scenes
➤ Mr Elton's proposal
➤ the Eltons and Harriet at the ball
➤ Emma's apology to Miss Bates after Box Hill

The Way Relationships Are Presented
➤ between Emma and Mr Woodhouse
➤ Frank's charming Emma / 'clues' about Jane
➤ between Emma and Mr Knightley

Performances/Casting

- Harriet (suitably dim-witted while at the same time capturing her tenderness of heart and lack of malice?)
- Mrs Elton (vulgarity and self-importance conveyed? a comic figure?)
- Miss Bates
- Mr Woodhouse
- Jane Fairfax (which actor best portrays her **reserve**? her feelings for Frank Churchill?)
- Emma: Consider these ideas from the makers of Version 2:

  Sometimes you want to hug her and sometimes you want to slap her. You can't quite work her out. . . . she's a real meddlesome nuisance and a difficult character . . . she really does mess people's lives up, nearly very seriously. But she changes at the end . . . just. (producer and director)

  She thinks she hasn't got a heart to break herself, and it's only about seven-eighths of the way through the film that she realises that she's just as vulnerable as any body else. I think that's when we really start to love her. (scriptwriter)

  How well do these comments describe Austen's character? Are these qualities conveyed in all versions?

4. **FILM *Clueless* Starring Alicia Silverstone**

*For broader-minded Janeites there has been the surprising pleasure of Hollywood's **Clueless**, based on **Emma** though set among the smugly rich of Beverly Hills, with the scrumptious mini-skirted Alicia Silverstone . . . as a campus Emma Woodhouse accessorised with mobile phone and gold credit card.* (James Hall *The Australian Magazine* Nov. 11-12 1995)

This description can be compared with the narrator's comments on Emma on the first page of the novel and Cher's American rich-girl lifestyle throughout the film can be seen as parallel to Emma's cocooned, complacent and privileged life in the little world of Highbury.

Students might enjoy detecting other 'correspondences':

A. CHARACTERS: Of whom are these modern counterparts?

- Tai, the 'clueless' new girl given a 'make-over' by Cher
- Travis, the good-hearted, socially unacceptable skateboarder
- Josh, Cher's older (college-age) 'ex-step-brother'
- Elton, the self-centred boy chosen by Cher for Tai
- Christian, the smooth charmer on whom Cher has a crush
- Amber, Cher's rival
- Cher's father who has to watch his cholesterol and 'eat right'

- the maid from El Salvador upset when Cher calls her Mexican

B. PLOT DETAILS: – modern versions of these Austen episodes?

- Mr Elton's praise for Emma's portrait of Harriet
- the frequent disagreements of Emma and Mr Knightley
- Frank Churchill's moving between the Churchills and the Westons
- Emma and Mr Elton alone in the carriage – his marriage proposal
- Mr Knightley's jealousy coinciding with the arrival of Frank (+ his later suspicion)
- Frank Churchill's secret (imposed by the attitudes of his society)
- Mr Knightley's dancing with Harriet at the ball
- Frank Churchill's rescue of Harriet from the gypsies
- Emma's facing the fact that **Harriet from being humble** has **grown vain**
- Emma's emotional turmoil after Mr Knightley reproaches her for insulting Miss Bates
- Emma's sudden realisation that she loves Mr Knightley.

Other examples?

C. LANGUAGE AND STYLE

- The last example (above) contains a rare use of figurative language by Austen — *It darted through her with the speed of an arrow, that Mr Knightley must marry no one but herself!* Discussion might explore the way this is translated into a visual effect: Cher's voice-over *"Then, suddenly – I love Josh!"* as simultaneously the fountain in the background lights up pink.
- The following might be compared with Austen's language at similar stages of the novel:
  - Cher's praise for Tai's appearance as she photographs her: *like one of those Botticelli chicks*
  - Elton's expression of snobbery when Cher rejects him: *Me and Tai don't make sense. Me and you make sense*
  - Josh criticising Cher: says Tai is *your Barbie doll* / after the 'Miss Bates insult' *You're such a brat*
  - Murray's way of telling Cher that Christian is gay: *He's a disco-dancing, Oscar-Wilde-reading, Streisand-ticket-holding, friend of Dorothy.*
  - Tai, newly confident and keen on Josh: *Am I some sort of mentally challenged air-head? I'm not good enough for Josh or something? You're a virgin who can't drive!* (Is Austen's Harriet so aggressive?)
- The film's use of Cher's voice-over narration may be seen as corresponding to two of the novel's narrative methods — the presentation of most events through Emma's eyes and the use of irony to emphasise her lack of awareness.
  The viewer is often given an ironic contrast between Cher's point of view and what is presented visually by the camera.
  - in the opening sequence: *I actually have a way normal life for a teenage girl. I get up, I brush my teeth and I pick out my school clothes.* What shots accompany this?
  - at the party: *Love was everywhere* + images of prone teenagers vomiting in the swimming pool, staggering etc.
  Other examples?

D. SETTING AND SOCIAL COMMENT

Austen was a subtle and sometimes satirical observer of her society. The film (not so subtly) satirises Cher's world.

- ➤ the obsession with fashion and shopping (see the episode of Cher and the mugger)
- ➤ the use of mobile phones (teenagers and adults)
- ➤ Cher's idea of 'disaster relief' – donating red caviar and skis.
- ➤ ignorance of world events (Cher watching television).

Other examples?

E. THE ENDING

Cher's *Well, you can guess what happens next* – followed by a scornful *As if ! !* as bride and groom are revealed to be her middle-aged teachers (Mr and Mrs Weston from the novel's opening?)

Is this a comment on the expectations of modern women compared to women's roles in Jane Austen's world?

ADDENDUM

Alternative Page References Worksheets 1–4.

The following are page references for the Penguin Classics edition (published 1996.)

Worksheet 4: The Harriet Smith- Mr Elton Affair.

4. References: Ch 6: p37, p38, p40, pp40-43, Ch 7: p48, Ch 8: pp58-9, Ch 9, Ch 10: pp75-6, pp76-77, Ch 13: pp92-3, p94, pp95-7, Ch 14: pp98-100., Ch 15: pp104-5.
5. Passage For Close Reading Ch 15 p108 to p110
6. Quotation: p114; (b) p115.

Worksheet 5: The Jane Fairfax- Frank Churchill Episodes.

2. Ch 20: p180, pp139-141.
3. Ch 26 pp185- 190, Ch 33 pp 235-7, Ch 51 p368
4. Ch 33 p235, Ch 34 p245
5. Ch 50 p359
6. b) Ch 23 pp160-162, Ch 24 pp165-6, pp167-9 Ch 26 pp179-181, p184, p190, Ch 27 pp193-4 Ch 28 pp200-201, Ch 29 p210.
   c) Ch 24 pp166-7(c.f. Ch 25 p170), p168, Ch 26 pp178-9, p187,* Ch 27 pp195-8, Ch 28 p199, p201, Ch 30 p215, Ch 34 pp240ff, Ch 37 p262, Ch 38 p265, p268, * Ch 41 pp285-7, pp287ff,Ch 42pp300-302,Ch 43p303, pp307-8,* CH44 pp313-6.
   d) See references marked * above.
8. A Close Reading Of Chapter 41 pp 284 ff.

Worksheet 6: Humiliation -- and Self-Awareness?

1. Ch 37 p261,
2. a) Quotation = p277, Ch 47 p333-5,
   c) Quotation = p278, Ch 40 esp. p282-3, p328, Ch 47 p331.
3. a) Ch 38 pp270-1, p273
4. Ch 46 p325-6 Ch 47 p331, p332
5. Ch 47 pp337-8, pp339-40
10. Ch 47 pp335-6, pp339-40
11. Ch 48 p341, pp 345-6
12. Ch 54 pp 385-8, p389

Worksheet 7: The Men in Emma's Life

4. b) Ch 49 pp 354-5
   c) Ch 49 pp554-5

Worksheet 9: The Comic Characters

2. b) ii) Passage For Close Reading: from Ch 42 p296 to pp297, p396.
   c) ii) Passage For Close Reading: from Ch 12 p85 to p89.

Jane Austen's

"Persuasion"

Persuasion – Contents

Section A:	**Setting and Social Groups**	**87**
Worksheet 1	The Society of Which	
	The Novel Gives a Picture	88
Worksheet 2	Place Settings	89
Worksheet 3	Social Groups or "Sets of People"	92
Section B:	**Plot / Structure**	**95**
Worksheet 4	The Novel's Opening	96
Worksheet 5	The Structure of the Novel as a Whole	97
Worksheet 6	The Revised Ending	101
Worksheet 7	Plot Mechanisms –	
	The Role of Various Characters	102
Section C:	**Ideas / Issues / Main Concerns**	**105**
Worksheet 8	Courtship and Marriage	106
Worksheet 9	The Novel's Title	107
Worksheet 10	"A Woman's Portion"	109
Worksheet 11	Change and Constancy	111
Worksheet 12	"Follies and Nonsense"	
	The Faults of Human Nature	112
Section D:	**The Heroine**	**113**
Worksheet 13	Characterisation and	
	Narrative Techniques	114
Suggestions for Further Reading and Viewing		**118**
Addendum: Alternative Page References		**121**
Comparison Questions		**122**

Section A:
SETTING AND
SOCIAL GROUPS

Worksheet 1
The Society Of Which
The Novel Gives a Picture

1. Jane Austen's world (the English countryside of the late 18th and early 19th Century) was very different from the world of the late 1990's / 21st Century. To appreciate the attitudes of the society depicted in her novels, some background reading is recommended. For example:
   - ▶ Fay Weldon *Letters To Alice: On First Reading Jane Austen* (in the form of letters by a modern 'feminist' novelist to an imaginary niece with green spiked hair.)
   - ▶ Christopher Gillie *A Preface To Jane Austen* (Chapter 9 *Women in Life and Literature*).
   - ▶ David Cecil *A Portrait Of Jane Austen* (particularly *Prologue: The World* and illustrations)
   - ▶ W A Craik *Jane Austen In Her Time.*
   - ▶ G M Trevelyan *A Social History Of England* Volume IV
   - ▶ Claire Tomalin *Jane Austen: A Life.*

2. In your reading of the novel itself be alert to details which throw light on the following:
   - ▶ The class system/the importance of property ("the landed gentry"); the landowner's responsibilities
   - ▶ The navy: paths to promotion and wealth; prize-money for capture of enemy ships.
   - ▶ Attitudes to marriage / single women and widows.
   - ▶ Insistence on manners and decorum e.g visiting code, forms of address, female behaviour.
   - ▶ Pastimes: visiting, dinner parties, card-playing, music, walking, hunting and shooting.
   - ▶ The 'season' in London or Bath/fashionable activities and 'social-climbing'.
   - ▶ Travel and communication/transport – carriages and sedan-chairs.

3. *The functioning of individuals while they are hemmed in by others, all mutually controlled by the system of social forces, was one of her general preoccupations. . . . A characteristic feature of which Jane Austen makes very frequent use was the large party in the same drawing room with the possibility of private conversations in an undertone, sometimes overheard, sometimes concealed by the conversation of others or the sound of the piano.* (D W Harding)
   In what ways do the following chapters show characters *hemmed in by others* and *controlled by social forces* or make use of conversations *overheard* or *concealed* during social occasions?
   a) Chapter 8 (the dinner party and dancing at Uppercross).
   b) Chapter 19 (at Molland's confectioner's shop in Milsom Street, Bath).
   c) Chapter 20 (the concert in Bath - the octagon room and the concert rooms).
   d) Chapter 22 (the **quick-changing unsettled scene** in the Musgroves' rooms in the White Hart hotel) pp226-231.
   e) Chapter 23 (at the White Hart again) pp233-242.
   f) Chapter 23 (the card party at Camden Place) pp247-248.

Worksheet 2
Place Settings

1. The Country — Kellynch Hall And Uppercross

Kellynch Hall

a) Brief descriptive details only are given of Sir Walter Elliot's country estate in Somersetshire. Using these details (Chapter 2 p44, Chapter 3 p48), write your own impression of Kellynch Hall (1 or 2 sentences).

b) Sir Walter's position as a member of the landed gentry owning such an estate carried responsibilities. His neglect of these is satirised by Jane Austen.
Find examples of language with an **ironic tone** used to comment on:

    I)   his management (with Elizabeth) of financial affairs. (Chapter 1 pp40-41)

    ii) his self-deception about his relationship with his tenantry. (Chapter 5 p63)
       (See Anne's judgement of Admiral Croft's management of the estate Chapter 13 pp140 ff and her thoughts in Ch 15, p152.)

Uppercross

c) What descriptive details are given of the Musgrove property at Uppercross? (Chapter 5 pp63 ff.)
NB: *"The Musgroves, like their houses were in a state of alteration, perhaps improvement"*. (p67) Significance?
(See Worksheet 11 4 (b)).

d) This setting places Anne amidst *"the influence so sweet and so sad of the autumnal months in the country"* (p61).
A feature of the country landscape on the walk from Uppercross to Winthrop in Chapter 10 is a hedgerow, a border of copse-wood or trees wide enough to enclose a winding path or cart track. How is this linked to an important plot episode?

e) I) Read the details given in Chapter 6 bottom p69 and pp73-4 and briefly sum up the way of life at Uppercross.

    ii) **Passage For Close Reading**
       from p148 *"The Musgroves came back"* to p149 *"not to call at Uppercross in the Christmas holidays"*.

How does Jane Austen's use of language create a humorous or ironic tone in this description of an Uppercross Christmas? Consider:
➤ selection of detail,
➤ arrangement of ideas,
➤ word choice,
➤ sentence structure.

2. The Seaside – Lyme Regis

Lyme Regis, Dorset

f) The seaside town, Lyme, (described Ch 11 p117) is associated with the return of Anne's *"bloom and freshness"* in contrast to her *"faded and thin"* looks at Kellynch.
Can you suggest any other explanation apart from the sea air?

g) *"Anne thought she left great happiness behind her when they quitted the house"*. (Chapter 11 p120) What details create this impression of the interior of Captain Harville's *"small house near the foot of an old pier?*

h) Enclosing the harbour of Lyme is a sea-wall or breakwater called the Cobb. Steep flights of steps at least six feet high lead from the higher level to the lower Cobb. To what key incident of the plot is this detail of setting crucial?

The curving wall of The Cobb at Lyme Regis protects the harbour and beaches from the might of the sea.

3. Bath – Fashionable Resort And Spa

> The city of Bath, mostly built between 1760 and 1810, was in its full bloom of fashion and beauty in Jane Austen's time and is still famous for its Georgian architecture. Originally popular as a spa to which people travelled for medical reasons to take a course of supposedly beneficial mineral waters (the name comes from the Roman baths over which the Georgian building known as the Pump Room is built), Bath became an alternative to London as a place to spend the 'season' – a less expensive place to lead a fashionable life. The 18th Century artist, Thomas Rowlandson, produced a famous set of drawings titled "The Comforts of Bath" which satirised the various types to be found in Bath society.

i)   Which characters are visiting Bath for medical reasons? (Chapter 17, p165 and Chapter 18, pp176-7) Which characters are there for social reasons?

j)   Compare Anne's **_disinclination for Bath_** with Lady Russell's attitude:

   i)   Find examples of language which presents in a tone of mild satire or amusement Lady Russell's rationalising of her partiality for Bath (Chapter 2 p45, p46; Chapter 14, p149.)

   ii) In the description of Anne and Lady Russell entering the city at the end of Chapter 14 (p149) how does the choice of language convey Anne's feelings about Bath?

k)   Sir Walter's main criticism of Bath (p155) is consistent with his characterisation throughout the novel. Explain.

*Milsom Street, from Nattes' **Bath**, 1806*

Worksheet 3
Social Groups or 'Sets of People'

The heroine mixes with three different sets of people. All these groups are brought together in the ending of the novel. Consider how each of these 'social circles' is related to some of the main concerns of *Persuasion*:

1. The Kellynch/Bath Circle

A deadening world of self-importance, self-seeking, snobbery and social-climbing.

a) What characters and episodes illustrate the above qualities throughout the novel? References?

(NB: Do not overlook Lady Russell who, despite her ability to value Anne, **had a value for rank and consequence, which blinded her a little to the faults of those who possessed them** (p42) and is very much part of the Bath circle.)

b) Jane Austen's judgement of Sir Walter and Elizabeth is indicated by her satirical tone in the opening Kellynch section. (See Worksheet 4 Q1)

   i) Find examples of a similar satirical treatment in the later Bath section.

   ii) Comment on the effect created by language used in the paragraph describing their entrance to the Musgroves' rooms in the White Hart hotel. (Chapter 22 p230 from **Their preparations** to **mortifying that it was so**!.)

c) What is Anne's judgement of the people her father and sister value most highly in this circle and of their fashionable activities in **the first set in Bath**? (Chapter 16, pp161-3; Chapter 19, p189.) Compare Lady Russell / Mr Elliot.

2. The Musgroves Of Uppercross

D W Harding points out that the Elliot pride and pretensions *based on family and superficial elegance* are contrasted with *the solid security of the Musgroves, undistinguished landowners, who look after their estates effectively* and Anne is shown to value the informal manners and warm-hearted family feeling of this group. Nevertheless Harding also says that while they are not as severely satirised as the Kellynch / Bath circle, Austen *remains a detached observer of the limitations of such people as she represents in the Musgroves* and Yasmine Gooneratne labels their world one of *self-centred benevolence*.

d) Find sections of the novel in which the Musgroves' limitations and their self-centred behaviour are revealed.
   References:
   Chapter 6, p69, p70, pp70-72, pp73-74, pp76-8 (+ Chapter 8, p89, pp91-92); Chapter 7, p80, pp80-83, Chapter 8, pp95-6; Chapter 10, pp108-9; Chapter 12, pp123-4

3. The Naval Circle

LEFT: A Lieutenant, and RIGHT: a Captain of the Royal Navy

> *. . . the story of **Persuasion** can be described not solely as the reconciliation of Anne and Wentworth, but also as the bursting open of the prison that Sir Walter and Elizabeth have made of Kellynch – the expansion of her world. In **Persuasion** the opening shows us the Kellynch party significantly grouped. . . . They seem immovable; but presently the Crofts begin to be heard of, and a fresher air stirs – faintly at first, but when they actually appear, irresistibly, for light as it is it has crossed the Atlantic.* (Mary Lascelles)

e) i) In the chapter in which the Crofts are introduced (Chapter 3) Sir Walter's attitude to the navy (p49) is used to comment satirically on his own character. Explain.
How does this humorous dialogue also suggest changing social values?
(See also Worksheet 11 Q4.)

ii) Find evidence of the qualities which lead to Anne's admiration and affection for Admiral and Mrs Croft:
(Chapter 3 p52; Chapter 8 pp92-5; Chapter 10 p107, p114; Chapter 13 pp141-3; Chapter 18 p174, pp178-80.)

f) J F Burrows says *if Sir Walter and Elizabeth are shown at their most characteristic in the sterile glitter of Bath, the naval officers are shown to advantage in their snug quarters at Lyme Regis, within sight of their beloved sea.*

i) Captain Harville's house at Lyme had **rooms so small as none but those who invite from the heart could think capable of accommodating so many** (Ch 11, p119). Explain what Anne means when she compares **the usual style of give-and-take invitations and dinners of formality and display** in her social circle with this hospitality.

ii) In particular compare Elizabeth Elliot's issuing of invitations to Camden Place in the later Bath section. (Chapter 22, pp 224-5, pp 230-231.)

iii) Compare the language used to describe the simplicity and warmth of Captain and Mrs Harville with Anne's judgement of Mr Elliot in Bath. (Chapter 17, p173 beginning **Mr Elliot was rational, discreet, polished.**)

g) While Anne's regretful thoughts at Lyme – **These would have been all my friends** – (p119) are kept to herself, Louisa's praises of **the character of the navy** are very definitely voiced (p120).

i) Comment on the cumulative effect created by the following examples of Austen's language: **burst forth, raptures of admiration and delight, protesting, convinced, only they** (repetition), **deserved, respected, loved.**

ii) Nevertheless is there evidence in this and other sections of the novel that the naval characters do possess the qualities of **friendliness, brotherliness, openness,** and **uprightness**?

h) Captain Wentworth is the main representative of the naval officers in the novel. What is the importance of:

i) his energy, self-reliance, and faith in individual achievement?

ii) the fact that Anne at the end of the novel **gloried in being a sailor's wife**[1]?

---

1   Compare Elizabeth's move to Pemberley in the more conservative ending of *Pride and Prejudice* which supports established social patterns. Anne has *"no Uppercross Hall before her, no landed estate".*

Section B:
PLOT / STRUCTURE

Worksheet 4
The Novel's Opening

1. The novel begins not with the heroine but with Sir Walter Elliot.

   Consider the idea that this introduction *indicates at once, and largely through its tone, that a trait of personality is being as sharply and mockingly emphasised as the nose or eyebrows of a politician in a cartoon.*

   The initial account of Sir Walter Elliot's vanity about his rank and personal appearance concludes **'He considered the blessing of beauty as inferior only to the blessing of a baronetcy; and the Sir Walter Elliot who united these gifts was the constant object of his warmest respect and devotion.'** *Not only the exaggeration, but the tone of ironic mockery in describing a defect of personality announces the intention of caricature.* (D W Harding)

   a) Examine the opening paragraphs (up to quoted section). By what methods is this *tone of ironic mockery created*?

   b) i) List all the details from the early chapters (1-5) which reinforce this opening impression of pride and vanity as Sir Walter's dominating character traits.

   ii) How are his pride and vanity used to **persuade** him to a sensible solution of his financial problems?

   c) What amusing reminder of Sir Walter's vanity can you find in Chapter 13 (ie, long after he has moved to Bath and ceased to play a major role in Volume 1)?

2. Consider Jane Austen's initial presentation of Sir Walter's eldest and youngest daughters. In what ways does each reflect the Elliot pride emphasised in the opening character sketch of their father?

3. *A very great deal of Jane Austen's effort in this novel is devoted to communicating, with sympathy and immediacy, the emotional side of her heroine's nature. Our sympathy and understanding are won for Anne from the very beginning because we share her station of passive listener and observer throughout the brilliant opening description of her father's religious reverence for the commandments of rank as embodied in that 'book of books', the Baronetage; and again, during the conversations with Mr Shepherd, the lawyer, that rapidly succeed it, concerning the letting of Kellynch Hall.* (Yasmine Gooneratne)

   a) Examine the description of Anne Elliot in Chapter 1. Note the mixture of viewpoints:
   - authorial comment;
   - the judgement of Sir Walter and Elizabeth;
   - Lady Russell's view.
   What opening impression of Anne is left with the reader ?

   b) It is not till Chapter 3 that Anne's quiet voice is heard for the first time; ***Here Anne spoke,*** – (top of p49). From your knowledge of the rest of the novel, especially Chapter 4, what significance can you find in:
   i) what Anne says in Chapter 3;
   ii) the conclusion of Chapter 3 – Anne's ***flushed cheeks***?

Worksheet 5
The Structure Of The Novel As a Whole

The structure of the novel is a simple one – concerned only to bring Anne Elliot and Captain Wentworth together. The novel falls into two sections.

In the first..., Anne, always in the background, is forced to witness Wentworth's courtship of Louisa Musgrave. In the second, the situation is reversed and Wentworth is witness to Mr Elliot's courtship of Anne..

The climax to the first part comes with Louisa Musgrove's accident on the Cobb at Lyme.. It is this accident which makes Wentworth realise he still loves Anne. The climax of the second part comes with his overhearing Anne's spirited defence of women's constancy in love, which persuades him that she might still love him. (Norman Sherry)

GROUP WORK: The First Section

1. What is Anne's attitude to Wentworth at the age of twenty-seven, eight years after her rejection of his proposal? (Chapter 4) Use page references / quotations to support your answer.

2. What coincidences / chance combinations of events lead to their meeting again ? What does Sherry mean when he says *The Elliot pride which drove the lovers apart is now the means of bringing them together.*?

3. Examine carefully the section immediately before their reunion (Ch 6: p75, p77; Ch 7: p79, p80, pp83-4) **and** the description of their meeting (Chapter 7 pp84-85).

    a) What is revealed about Anne by her thoughts and feelings as she anticipates seeing Wentworth again ?

    b) **Passage For Close Reading.**
    (from ***Mary, very much gratified*** to ***the folly which asked the question.*** Chapter 7.)
    How does Austen's language and style, including the sentence structure and punctuation, convey Anne's feelings ?

4. What is revealed about
    a) Mary
    b) Anne
    in their reactions to Captain Wentworth's remark, ***You were so altered he should not have known you again.***?

5. At the end of Chapter 7 the focus moves from Anne to Captain Wentworth in the two paragraphs ending with the sentence ***Her power with him was gone forever***.
    a) Whose words are these: the narrator's? Wentworth's?
    (See also Chapter 8: ***It was a perpetual estrangement***. Whose view is this?)
    b) *Has* Wentworth succeeded in forgetting Anne? Discuss the evidence for / against in this chapter and the rest of the first section (to end of Chapter 12).

6. Despite the words quoted in Q 5, Andrew H Wright says *No reader can be in doubt . . . as to the final outcome; but, as the essence of suspense is waiting for the expected, the succeeding chapters are read with mounting interest – for we wonder how the lovers will, at last, be re-united. There are many difficulties to overcome.* Using the references below, list the sequence of incidents by which the emotional barriers Wentworth has erected against Anne are gradually broken down.

   ▶ Before you begin, think about this comment by Mary Lascelles on the way most of these incidents are seen from Anne's point of view:
   We share her alternating moods of confidence and diffidence as to her power to read Wentworth's manner and actions; with her we sometimes overhear words of his that seem to bear a meaning beyond that addressed to the immediate listener; or hear his friends' account of his intentions, wondering how much it is worth.

   ▶ Consider each incident from the point of view of Anne's "alternating moods" but also decide, in retrospect, what Jane Austen is saying about Wentworth's attitude in each case.

In another moment . . . someone was taking him from her.

   References: Chapter 8: pp88-9, p92, pp95-6; Chapter 9: pp98-100, pp102-4 Chapter 10: pp106-7, pp109-110, p111, pp112-113, pp113-114, Chapter 11: p115; p119; Chapter 12: pp124-5.

7. Discuss all the uses Austen makes of the incident which is the climax of this first section - Louisa Musgrove's fall from the Cobb, the sea wall at Lyme. (See Worksheet 2.) Make notes on the significance of this episode for the novel as a whole.
   References: Chapter 12 p129 ff. especially pp133-4, p135.

   (Think about characterisation and main concerns or themes as well as plot.)

8. *Although suspense and strong emotion are maintained to the last pages, the visit to Lyme is the turning point at which the earlier sadness – wasted opportunity, regret, misunderstanding – has finally been modulated with infinite skill into comedy. – The mingling of tones is seen at its boldest in the climax, the accident on the Cobb, where elements of comedy are deliberately introduced into what is primarily a scene of shock and anxiety and family disaster.* (D W Harding)

a) How are qualities already established in the characters of Anne's companions used for overtones of comedy?

b) Yasmine Gooneratne says the absurd behaviour of the whole party is a weakness of the novel. Do you agree?

c) Consider the following reading:

The horror of the moment to all who stood around!

And then, in the close of the episode, a familiar voice penetrates the babble of the poor Musgroves, a voice which no one who has heard it before can fail to recognise as Jane Austen's own: **By this time the report of the accident had spread among the workmen and boatmen about the Cobb, and many were collected near them, to be useful if wanted, at any rate, to enjoy the sight of a dead young lady, nay, two dead young ladies, for it proved twice as fine as the first report.** *The mockery sheathed in that phrase* **nay, two dead young ladies** *pricks in an instant the bubble catastrophe; for its import is perfectly clear to anyone who has observed Jane Austen's dealings with her readers. She will not allow them to misapprehend, here, the nature of the castrophe. It is a climax to the earlier part of the action in that it brings to a head, and solves, a problem which that had set – the knot tied by Wentworth's fanciful preference for Louisa, her fanciful infatuation with him. But the catastrophe which the spectators think they are witnessing is an illusion. Louisa is not dead... True she has fallen on her head; but it had never been a very good one, and the blow seems to have cleared it – for she acquires a taste for poetry and learns to attach herself to a man who can return her affection. And yet Mr Read[1] offers this scene as an example of Jane Austen's failure in serious emotional writing. Her style, he complains "becomes almost ludicrous... under the strain of dramatic action," and he quotes a passage from this episode and goes on to pick from it phrases "which are not congruous with the tragedy of the situation". Moreover he contrasts with its insignificance the urgency of the scene in which Heathcliff[2] is found dead – a real with a counterfeit catastrophe. His quotation, however, stops short of the two dead young ladies, and so misses the key to the ironical tone of the episode.* (Mary Lascelles)

9. a) Has Captain Wentworth's opinion of Anne already changed before the end of Chapter 12? Evidence?

b) How does she misread his behaviour after the accident?
References: Chapter 12: p132, p135, p136. (Also Volume 2? Chapter 13: p141, Chapter 14: p147)

c) Consider the paragraph beginning **Anne wondered whether it ever occurred to him now** (end of Chapter 12). How does this show that she is human, not saintly or perfect?

1   Herbert Read, *Enlish Prose Style* (1928) pp119-120.
2   Heathcliff: character in Emily Bronte's tragic novel, *Wuthering Heights*.

10. a) Sum up Anne's state of mind as she leaves Uppercross at the beginning of the second stage of the plot-Volume 2. (Chapter 13 – from p138 *If Louisa recovered* to p139 *that such things had been*.) How is the description of the weather attuned to her mood ? How accurate is her assessment of the situation?

   b) Compare the conclusion of Chapter 13. How seriously does the narrator mean us to take these assurances? Comment on the **tone** created by words such as ***danger***, ***safe***, and ***smiled***.

GROUP WORK: The Second Section

Read the summary of the structure of Volume 2 at the beginning of this Worksheet:

1. Trace the changing attitudes/feelings of Anne and Wentworth through the difficulties and misunderstandings of this second Volume to the climax in Chapter 23.
   References:
   Before Anne leaves Uppercross and Kellynch:
   Chapter 13,   p138, p140, pp141-2, p143; Chapter 14, p147.
   In Bath:
   Chapter 18   (Mary's letter) especially pp177-8, pp180-183.
   Chapter 19   (first meeting since Lyme) pp185-7, pp188-9, p189.
   Chapter 20   (the concert) pp191-5, pp197-8, pp198-199.

   Chapter 21   (after the concert) p200, p204
   Chapter 22   (at the White Hart after Mrs Smith's revelations)
                 p226, p227, pp228-9, pp229-230, pp230-231.
   Chapter 23   (at the White Hart next day – Anne's conversation with Captain Harville)
                 p233, pp 234 - 35, pp235 - 8, pp239- 40, pp241 - 242.

2. In retrospect is it possible to place a different interpretation from the misconstructions of Anne and/or Wentworth on their actions and reactions? (Compare your own impressions of the events of Volume 1 and Volume 2 on first reading with Wentworth's summary in Chapter 23 pp243-7)

Worksheet 6
The Revised Ending

> Jane Austen was not satisfied with her original ending and re-wrote it. Read the cancelled chapter (printed pp 255 ff Penguin edition[1].), noting the way it brought the lovers together. Compare Chapters 22 and 23 of the final version and decide what Jane Austen achieved by the changes she made:

1. The first ending had Admiral Croft bringing Anne and Wentworth together[2] in circumstances in which Anne's role in their reconciliation was a passive one. In Chapters 22 and 23 of the final version she plays a much more active role in ending their misunderstanding of each other's feelings. Explain this difference. Which version makes the better resolution to the plot complications discussed in Worksheet 5?

Select a quotation from Chapter 23 as a caption for this illustration from the 1890 edition of the novel.

"...
....
....
....
...."

2. The revised chapters also introduce a more extended discussion (end Chapter 23) of the issue in the novel's title. Discuss the significance of this concluding emphasis on the problem of the rights and wrongs of Anne's yielding to Lady Russell's persuasion. (See also Worksheet 9)

3. Despite the serious issues dealt with in the conclusion, the episode of the Musgroves' visit to Bath which Jane Austen added to these chapters allowed her to include more comedy and satire. Find examples of:
   a) comedy in the frustrating of Anne's attempts to communicate with Wentworth by the good-natured Musgroves;
   b) further comic treatment of the characters and relationship of Mary and Charles;
   c) further illustration of the Elliot snobbery and the narrator's attitude to this.

1   Also available on website www.pemberley.com
2   Roger Michell's 1995 film combines elements of both endings.

Worksheet 7
Plot Mechanisms – the Role of Various Characters

1. What is the role of **Captain Benwick** in Volume 2?
   References: Chapter 14, Chapter 18, Chapter 22, Chapter 23.

2. Consider **Mr Elliot**'s role in the novel:

   a) In the opening chapter the *Baronetage* establishes him as Sir Walter's heir (NB: despite three daughters). What reasons are given for his estrangement from the family and the resentment of Sir Walter and Elizabeth?

   b) Mr Elliot is not heard of again until Ch 12 – at Lyme.

   They ascended and passed him. - - - It was evident that the gentleman admired her exceedingly. Captain Wentworth looked round at her instantly in a way which shewed his noticing of it.

   What are the reactions of i) Mary, ii) Anne, iii) Wentworth to this encounter?

   c) How do the attitudes of the following characters change towards Mr Elliot in Bath?
      ➤ Sir Walter and Elizabeth (Ch 14, p150; Ch 15 pp152-4)
      ➤ Lady Russell (Ch 14 p147, p150; Ch 16 p159-60; Ch 17 p171, p173)
      ➤ even Anne (Ch 15 pp156-7, Ch 17 p172, Ch 20 pp195-7) though despite his charm and elegance her initial reservations (Ch 15 p153) remain (Ch 17 p172-3) and his attentions cause problems (Ch 19 pp184-7, p199)

   d) Is the reader adequately prepared for his "unmasking" (Ch 21) and his liaison with Mrs Clay (Ch 24)?
      (See Q3.)

3. a) Mrs Clay is described in Ch 21 as *a clever, insinuating, handsome woman, poor and plausible*. Find evidence of:
    - her skill at flattering and ingratiating herself with Sir Walter and Elizabeth;
    - growing concern of Anne, Lady Russell and Mr Elliot over her scheming to become Sir Walter's wife.

    References: Ch 2, p46; Ch 3 p48-50; Ch 5 pp61-2, Ch 16, p158, Ch17, p170; Ch 22, p220; Ch 15 p151; Ch 16 p158, p159, p163; Ch 17 p173; Ch 21 pp212-4.

    b) Mrs Clay's transferring of her interest in Sir Walter to Mr Elliot is announced in Ch 24 p252. Is this surprising for a reader ? Are there clues (if we are not focusing as Anne is on other things)?

    How clearly are Mr Elliot's motives presented?

    References: Ch 19 pp184-5, p187; Ch 22 p227, p232.

GOWLAND'S LOTION IMPROVED,
By Macdonald (from Dickinson's,) prepared only by
MACDONALD, HUMBERT, & CO.
At their Royal Arcanum Warehouse, 53, Longacre,
AT REDUCED PRICES, VIZ.
Quarts, Pints, and Half Pints, 6s. 3s. 9d. and
2s. 3d. duty included.

To Gowland's Lotion now my muse has wing,
Its real intrinsic worth I mean to sing :
Long has it stood the foremost in the race
Of cosmetics, to beautify the face :
Eruptive humours fly before its power,
Pimples and freckles die within an hour.
Dread foe to beauty, thy disgusting harms
No more shall prey upon the ladies' charms ;
No more shall scrophula with horror creep,
And steal the beauty from the blooming cheek.
While Britons patronize each good invention,
This grand restorative must claim attention :
The best prepared, as chemic art can prove,
Once try'd, will every prejudice remove.
Who wants to see its true and genuine maker,
Must call at No. 53, Longacre.

∴ The Proprietors respectfully inform the public, that they can only be responsible for the good effects and efficacy of the *improved Lotion* : you are requested to ask for that only, or the Emollient Preventive. To be had at the Warehouse, and of every Vender in the united kingdom.

Advertisement for Gowland's Lotion.
Ackermann's Repository. November 1809

*Mrs Clay's **freckles** are part of Austen's satirical treatment
of Sir Walter's obsession with appearance (See Ch 16, pp158-9)*

4. a) Many readers see **Mrs Smith** as a weakness in the novel, a clumsy plot mechanism to reveal Mr Elliot's villainy. What do we learn of his real character in Ch 21 (p205 ff)? Are his motives made clear by Mrs Smith's account? How convincing is her reason for not revealing this to Anne earlier (p216) ?

   b) Is Mrs Smith also used to show qualities of Anne's character?
   Compare Anne's visits to her with the visits made by Sir Walter and Elizabeth as part of the social code (Ch 17 pp169-70)

Section C:
IDEAS / ISSUES /
MAIN CONCERNS

Worksheet 8
Courtship and Marriage

1. The poet W H Auden wrote about Jane Austen,

    "It makes me feel uncomfortable to see

    An English spinster of the middle-class

    Describe the amorous effects of 'brass',   'brass' = slang for 'money'

    Reveal so frankly and with such sobriety

    The economic basis of society."

    How does the phrase *the amorous effects of 'brass'* apply to courtship and marriage in
    Persuasion?

2. a) What attitudes to marriage are shown by the following characters?

Sir Walter	**Elizabeth**
Mary	**Lady Russell**
Henrietta	**Louisa**
Captain Benwick	**Mr Elliot**
Anne	**Captain Wentworth**

    Support what you say with evidence / page references.

    b) Consider each of the following marriages.
        Which are presented as 'good' marriages? Why?

    Sir Walter and Anne's Mother
    Admiral and Mrs Croft
    Mary and Charles Musgrove
    Captain and Mrs Harville
    Louisa and Captain Wentworth
    Louisa and Captain Benwick
    Anne and Mr Elliot
    Anne and Captain Wentworth.

3. Norman Sherry says of Austen's fiction

    *".... the romantic pattern of the novels, based upon the events of courtship and concluding with
    marriage, is a vehicle for serious moral problems which arise from the relationship of one human
    being with another. The novels involve us in a consideration of education, character, judgement,
    and right action, and while these are not the whole concern of Jane Austen, they are certainly an
    important concern."*

    How well does this comment apply to **Persuasion**?

Worksheet 9
The Novel's Title

1. *The word persuasion echoes throughout the novel of that title just as it is constantly haunting Anne Elliot. – It is as if she cannot get away from what she has done in allowing herself to be persuaded not to marry Frederick Wentworth – or dissuaded from marrying him.* (Tony Tanner)

   Persuasion *has one of those titles that echoes throughout the work it describes. And its range of meanings varies widely, from conveying a sense of coercion and duress to delicate, scarcely perceptible intimations of right conduct such as Anne Elliot offers to Captain Benwick.* (Michael Orange)

   a) How many mentions of the word **persuasion** can you find? (include verb forms 'to persuade', 'persuaded' etc.)
   b) How many different kinds of persuasion can you identify?

2. In the opening chapters the attitude of Sir Walter and Elizabeth to Anne means that it is Lady Russell and the lawyer, Mr Shepherd, who persuade them to economise. (See Worksheet 4).

   At Uppercross, however, Anne is often shown using quiet skill at persuading or being given the role of persuader for other people's convenience.

   Consider Ch 6 pp71-2; Ch 7 pp82-3 *

   (* Is there some self-deception here in Anne's being ***quite unpersuadable***?

   What other motives influence her as well as consideration for Charles and Mary?)

3. Louisa Musgrove has ***no idea of being . . . easily persuaded.***
   What use is made of this in the novel?

   References: Ch 10 from p109 ***Anne, really tired herself*** to ***give her extreme agitation.***

   Ch 12 from p129 ***There was too much wind*** to ***taken up lifeless.***

   Ch 12 from p135 ***Don't talk of it, he cried*** to ***a very resolute character.***

   Ch 23 from p244 ***At Lyme, he had received lessons*** to ***a collected mind.***

   Consider how the 'persuasion' theme is presented in the above sections:
   ➤ dramatically through characters, action and dialogue?
   ➤ directly by the narrator?
   ➤ Whose point of view is presented?
   ➤ Is an argument conveyed by the narrator's tone of sympathy or irony?

4. In a conversation at the beginning of Ch 12 Henrietta shows a strong desire to persuade the clergyman, Dr Shirley, to leave his parish at Uppercross and retire to Lyme, claiming her motive for such persuasion is concern for his health. Why is Anne amused?
   (Note: As a young clergyman Charles Hayter needs the income from a 'living' to marry.)

5.	In Ch 10 Louisa tells Captain Wentworth of the Musgroves' belief that when Charles proposed Lady Russell persuaded Anne to refuse him and in Ch 12 Henrietta says of Lady Russell *I always look upon her as able to persuade a person to any thing*!

D W Harding sums up the central problem announced by the title as *the rights and wrongs of Lady Russell's persuasion and of Anne's yielding.*

Debate these "rights and wrongs" (ie, decide what attitude you think Jane Austen is supporting) after considering all the sections of the novel listed below.

NB: Be aware of the point-of-view (Anne's? Wentworth's? Lady Russell's? the narrator's?) and of language and tone.

References:

Volume 1:	Ch 4 from p55 *A short period of exquisite felicity* to *the natural sequel of an unnatural beginning.*

Ch 7 from p86 *Frederick Wentworth had used such words* to *It had been weakness and timidity.*

Volume 2:	Ch 17 from p171 *Lady Russell was now perfectly decided* to *the course of the following autumn.*

{Ch 20 from p197 *The first act was over* to *that she had seen him.*
{Ch 23 from p246 *To see you, cried he* to *to believe her of less authority now.*

Ch 21 from p216 *Anne could just acknowledge* to *might have been persuaded by Lady Russell !*

Ch 23 from p248 *I have been thinking over the past* to *the accent was decisive enough.*

Ch 24 from p250 *The only one among them* to *take up a new set of opinions and hopes.*

6.	*But how important finally is the idea of persuasion in this novel ? As an issue it seems after the early chapters to have shifted from the centre of the novel. For as the novel develops, what does interest us (and, I suspect, Jane Austen) is not so much the abstract problem of how compliant an individual ought to be to the dictates of others, as the terms upon which Anne Elliot can achieve fulfilment in her particular world. . . . . The issue of fulfilment with its accompanying questions of responsibility is developed and explored in the novel with sensitivity and perception. . . . . But in spite of the happy ending, there is a melancholy sense both of time passing and the fragility of human happiness. Even in the moment of their reconciliation, Anne and Wentworth are conscious of many, many years of division and estrangement. Captain Wentworth comes back and Anne is given her opportunity to assert herself and reach out for her own happiness; but what if he had not? It seems to me that Jane Austen is as much concerned with questioning the possibilities of happiness for someone like Anne Elliot as dealing with the more abstract problems of behaviour implied in the title; and running counterpoint to the story of fulfilled love is an awareness that life is not often as generous as this in offering second chances.* (Jan Fox)

Do **you** think the idea of persuasion is the novel's central issue?

Worksheet 10
"A Woman's Portion"

> **"We live at home, quiet, confined..."** (Anne to Captain Harville Chapter 23)
>
> The 'persuasion' theme is linked with the idea of a woman's duty and the limitations – economic, educational, social – placed upon women by society. The possibility of happiness in such a society for an intelligent, sensitive woman is a concern throughout Jane Austen's novels but it is in *Persuasion* that these ideas are most explicitly analysed.

1. In the light of the pressures connected with marriage, comment on:

   a) the phrase **"the years of danger"** applied to Elizabeth in Chapter 1 and her attitude to the **"Baronetage"**;

   b) evidence of Mary's feelings of superiority to her older sisters;

   c) the role of Anne as a single woman - especially in the Uppercross section of the novel;

   d) Wentworth's phrase **"the horrible eligibilities and proprieties of the match"** (p246.)

2. Rules of social decorum placed many constraints on female behaviour. Consider:

   a) Wentworth's awareness that he was bound **"in honour"** to Louisa (Chapter 23 p245).

   b) Anne's attempts to communicate with or 'encourage' Wentworth:
   - at the concert (Chapter 20 pp198-9)
   - via the Musgroves (Chapter 22 p229, Chapter 23 pp24-2.).

   c) Mrs Smith's dependence on a man (Mr Elliot or Captain Wentworth) to recover her husband's property.

   d) The method by which Anne finally reveals her feelings to Wentworth in Chapter 23. Why can **she** not write to **him**?

3. In *A Vindication Of The Rights Of Women* (1792) Mary Wolllstonecraft challenged the idea that qualities such as submissiveness and docility were innate in women and that they did not have the same intellectual capacities or powers of reasoning as men. She argued that it was the lack of an education allowing them *to unfold their own faculties which made women want to be ladies. Which is simply to have nothing to do . . ..*

   a) Quote from Anne's debate with Captain Harville (Chapter 23, p237) words in which she expresses a similar idea.

   b) How does Mrs Croft's character support Wollstonecraft's views? (Ch 3, p52; Ch 8, pp93-5[1]; Ch 18, p179)

   c) Mary often behaves like a **fine lady** rather than a **rational creature**. Examples? Page references?

1 Places Mrs Croft calls "about home" – Ireland, Portugal, Gibraltar – would be far away to the other women listening.

4. Penny Gay says the changes made to the final chapters present Anne as *an effective and articulate feminist heroine.*

   a) How is the idea of a male-dominated literary tradition brought into her debate with Captain Harville in Chapter 23?

   b) The feminist critics Sandra M Gilbert and Susan Gubar point to the fact that the **Baronetage** which represents patriarchal culture in the opening of the novel reappears in the final chapter and claim that Anne can only replace this with the **Navy Lists**, a book in which women are conspicuously absent.
   How important do you think this is?

5. Consider the following reading, based on Anne's words in Chapter 23 (from **I have been thinking over the past** to **a woman's portion**).

   Now that her story has a happy ending Anne can afford to be generous. Now that her own desires are fulfilled, she can afford to assert the importance of duty to society. But the reader is very unlikely to agree with her judgement since the whole novel seems to have been concerned to point out what a waste her life would have been if Captain Wentworth had not happened to return to Kellynch. There is an apparent desire for compromise between elements which have been opposed in the course of the novel- the demands of the individual and those of society — elements which, we suspect, can't be so easily reconciled. Anne's story could so easily have been tragic and, had that been the case, she might have been less willing to defend women's 'duty'. (Vivien Jones)

   Do you agree?

   How convincing is Austen's presentation of Anne's attitude?

Worksheet 11
Change and Constancy

1. **Anne's Changing Appearance**.

   a) Eight years after breaking her engagement to Wentworth Anne has become *faded and thin* and, as Mary tactlessly reports, *so altered that he should not have known her again* Of what inner emotional state is this an outward sign?

   b) Trace the stages by which she gains a second spring of youth and beauty during the course of the novel. References p125; p139; p158; p187; p194; p247.

2. **Changing Seasons**

   Through the novel references to the seasons remind us of the passing of time and the changes it brings. Identify these. Chapter/Page references?

3. **Changing Relationships**

   "I do not think I ever opened a book in my life which had not something to say upon woman's inconstancy. Songs and proverbs, all talk of woman's fickleness." (Ch 23)

   What does Austen say in her book about women's constancy — and men's?

   a) How does the changeability of the Musgrove sisters highlight the constancy of Anne's feelings for Wentworth? Details? Chapter/Page references?

   b) Comment on the reactions of the following characters to the *"heart-broken"* Captain Benwick and his recovery from his *"inconsolable"* loss:
      ► Mary (Chapter 14, pp145-7; Chapter 18, p176)
      ► Admiral Croft (Chapter 18 p183)
      ► Captain Wentworth (Chapter 20 p192)
      ► Captain Harville (Chapter 23 pp235-8)
      ► Anne (Ch 11 pp121-2; Ch12 p127-8,p129; Ch 14, pp145-8, Ch 18, p176-8; Ch 23, pp235-8)

   c) Compare Wentworth's passionate declaration in his letter (Ch 23 p240) that he was *"never inconstant"* with his admission that he was *"constant unconsciously . . . unintentionally"*. (p244). – *"Anne smiled"* (p245). Why? (See p86)

4. **A Changing Society?**

   a) Jane Austen's other novels present a fixed social order. Most critics find *Persuasion* distinct from them in presenting a society which is changing. Consider how:
      ► the naval characters and in particular Wentworth's changing fortunes,
      ► the novel's ending,
      may be seen as used to suggest changing social values.

   b) What evidence is there that the Musgroves are presented as more capable than Sir Walter of adapting to change?

Worksheet 12
"Follies and Nonsense" The Faults of Human Nature

"Follies and nonsense, whims and inconsistencies diverted Elizabeth Bennet, and the same may be said of Jane Austen . . . and . . . it is this characteristic of seeing the inconsistencies and incongruities in life, the incongruity between a person's pretensions and his abilities, between his words and his actions, that makes her primarily a comic writer." (Norman Sherry)

The following human weaknesses are exposed in **Persuasion** –
some glanced at lightly in passing, others given more detailed comic or satirical treatment.

What characters and episodes exemplify these?

➤ pride and snobbery

➤ social climbing

➤ flattery / hypocrisy / duplicity

➤ vanity

➤ sentimentality and self-indulgence

➤ self-deception

➤ hypochondria and self-pity

➤ selfishness and self-interest

➤ greed and materialism

➤ tactlessness and insensitivity

➤ gossip and rumour / sensationalism

➤ obsession with sport

Can you suggest any others?

Section D:
THE HEROINE

Worksheet 13
Characterisation and Narrative Techniques

> The character of Anne Elliot is central to *Persuasion*. It is from her perspective, coloured by her feelings and judgements, that most of the events of the novel are presented.[1]
>
> Thus this worksheet focuses on the characterisation of Anne and techniques linked to this.
>
> With her quiet and self-effacing ways Anne is a very different character from the vivacious Elizabeth Bennet of *Pride And Prejudice* or the confident Emma. Has Austen avoided making her insipid and successfully created a character ***"maintaining the loveliest medium of fortitude and gentleness"*** (Wentworth's words p244)?

1. "... only Anne"

a) The paragraph in Chapter 1 which concludes – *"she was only Anne"* is an example of Austen's technique of shifts in narrative viewpoint. Whose view is given in the quoted words? How is it countered

- ▶ in the same paragraph (p37) by authorial comment in the form of a brief character sketch

- ▶ by the satirical tone in which the holder of this view is treated in the whole opening section

- ▶ by Lady Russell's attitude to Anne in this section (Chapters 1-5)?

b) Anne's sadness, emotional isolation, and sense of herself as an outsider are conveyed through much of the novel.

> *"Her loneliness is accentuated... by the changes of scene as she moves from one set of people to another, only to find that each group is totally absorbed in itself and uninterested in the affairs of anyone else."* (Jan Fox)

i) Find evidence from different sections of the novel to support the above statements.

ii) Nevertheless she is not presented as self-pitying. Find examples of:

- ▶ her discipline and restraint as she attempts to control her feelings;

- ▶ her sense of the ridiculous prompting her to laugh (or smile quietly?) at herself as well as others.

---

1   Though be aware of Austen's narrative technique of shifting point of view – sometimes within a paragraph or from one sentence to another.

c) Though she seems passive and submissive to the will of others through much of novel, Anne is shown as

    i) possessing the resolution of a collected mind and capable of decisive action (Chapter 7, Chapter 12)

    ii) growing in confidence as the novel progresses. (Chapter 17, Chapter 20)

Use the references indicated and other examples of your own to illustrate these qualities.

d) Despite the quiet restraint of Anne's outward behaviour the reader is kept aware of her intense inner emotion.

    i) In many sections of the novel Austen gives us insight into her unspoken thought and feelings in what Norman Page calls *free indirect speech* in which *the ... advantages of both direct and indirect speech are combined to fashion a medium which brings the reader close enough to the character's consciousness to have a sense of something at times resembling interior monologue, yet at the same time preserves the kind of objectivity, and the frequent reminders of an impartial authorial presence, which makes explicit comment possible.*
Consider how the following examples illustrate this:
p85·from **Soon, however, she began to reason with herself** to **the folly which asked the question**.
p199 from **Jealousy of Mr Elliot** to **their evil was incalculable**. Find others.

    ii) In changing the original ending (Chapter 23) how did Austen allow Anne to express passionate feelings?

2. Anne — and Others

A favourable view of Anne is created by Austen's use of other characters.

Find evidence to illustrate the following:

a) In contrast to Sir Walter and Elizabeth — and even Lady Russell — Anne is shown to have superior principles and sound judgements.

b) Seeing her in the company of Mary or Louisa highlights the admirable qualities of her behaviour and character.

c) The restraint of her unspoken sorrow is emphasised by the self-deception of Mrs Musgrove's **large fat sighings** over her worthless son and Captain Benwick's self-indulgent 'poetical' grieving.

d) She values **the frank, the open-hearted, the eager character** rather than the elegant manners of Mr Elliot.

e) She likes the Crofts and the Harvilles and is liked by them.

3. Anne — and the Narrator

The fact that Anne is excluded from the very satirical treatment of other members of her family is obvious evidence that she is presented sympathetically. Nevertheless there **are** occasions when the narrator's tone towards her is one of detached amusement or gentle irony.

Consider:

a) **Chapter 10 (the walk to Winthrop)**

➤ p106 reason Anne gives for not withdrawing when she learns Wentworth is to be present + reasons added by narrator.

➤ p107 statement that ***it was not possible*** for Anne to avoid eavesdropping on Wentworth's ***conversation with either of the Miss Musgroves***.

➤ p107 the undermining of the melancholy tone of the ***musings and quotations*** about autumn by the paragraph following immediately on p108 in which the narrator tells us cheerfully that ***the ploughs at work, and the fresh-made path spoke the farmer, counteracting the sweets of poetical despondence, and meaning to have spring again***.

➤ (How are Henrietta and Louisa also the targets of the narrator's irony in the seemingly innocuous statement p108 that ***young men are, sometimes, to be met with strolling about near home***?)

b) **Chapter 13 (the concluding paragraph)**
How does the narrator suggest a little self-deception on Anne's part here?
Is she meant to be taken seriously? What words in particular signal an ironic tone?

c) **Chapter 19 (Wentworth in Bath)**

➤ The ironic tone is more heavily underlined in the following sentence (p185). ***She now felt a great inclination to go to the outer door; she wanted to see if it rained***. Explain how the context shows this.

➤ Later in this chapter (pp188-9) Anne's suspense as she waits in the company of Lady Russell for Wentworth to pass them in the street is brought to a comic anti-climax. Explain.

d) **Chapters 20 and 21 (the concert and after)**

➤ Comment on the tone created by the underlined phrase in ***by some other removals, and a little scheming of her own, Anne was enabled to place herself much nearer the end of the bench***. (p198)

➤ In the paragraph on p 200 beginning ***Prettier musings of high-wrought love*** what language in particular contributes to the hyperbole and thus creates an ironic tone?

ESSAY QUESTIONS

1. *Though* **Persuasion** *moves very quietly, without sobs and screams, in drawing-rooms and country lanes, it is yet amongst the most emotional novels in our literature.* (Reginald Farrer)
   Show whether you agree with the above comment, making close reference to the novel to support what you say.

2. *Despite her loneliness and low spirits, her quiet and self-effacing manner throughout most of the novel, Anne Elliot is not an insipid character.*
   Test this claim by examining the methods used by Jane Austen to make Anne a sympathetic heroine and assessing their success.

3. *In* **Persuasion** *the selfishness of human nature is revealed – through behaviour which is self-seeking, or self-absorbed, or self-deceptive.*
   How well does this sum up the view of human nature presented in the novel as a whole? Illustrate by close reference to specific characters and episodes and the author's narrative techniques and tone.

4. *In* **Persuasion** *Jane Austen seems preoccupied by change: a changing society, changing affections, physical changes of many kinds. Only Anne's feelings remain constant.*
   To what extent do you agree with this assessment of **Persuasion**?

5. **But I hate to hear you talking so, like a fine gentleman, and as if women were all fine ladies, instead of rational creatures.** (Mrs Croft to Captain Wentworth Chapter 8.)
   Discuss the importance of this distinction between fine ladies and rational creatures in the novel as a whole and illustrate by examining the characterisation of at least three women.

6. What is the importance of the naval characters in **Persuasion**?
   (Discuss Jane Austen's method of presenting them and their thematic importance)

7. Discuss the proposition that *Although much of the point of view in* **Persuasion** *may be surrendered to Anne Elliot, the narrator retains a firm ironical control.* (G A Wilkes)

8. "A social satire", "A serious comedy of personal relationships", "Above all, a love story".
   Considering each of the above, and referring closely to the novel, decide which best sums up **Persuasion**.

Suggestions For Further Reading And Viewing

Reading

The following critical works are referred to in this order in the worksheets:

D W Harding — Introduction to Penguin English Library edition *Persuasion* 1966

Mary Lascelles — *Jane Austen And Her Art* Oxford University Press 1939

J F Burrows — ***Persuasion*** *and its 'Sets of People'* (*Sydney Studies In English* 2 1976-7)

Yasmine Gooneratne — *Jane Austen* Cambridge University Press 1970

Norman Sherry — *Jane Austen* Evans Brothers 1966

Andrew H. Wright — *Jane Austen's Novels: A Study In Structure.* Chatto & Windus 1961

Tony Tanner — *Jane Austen - In Between:* ***Persuasion*** Macmillan London 1986.
Michael Orange — *Aspects of Narration in* ***Persuasion*** (*Sydney Studies In English* 15,1989-90)

Sandra M Gilbert} — *Jane Austen's Cover Story* (in *The Madwoman In The Attic: The Woman*
& Susan Gubar } — *Writer and the Nineteenth Century Literary Imagination*) Yale University Press 1979

Norman Page — *The Language Of Jane Austen* Basil Blackwell 1972

Jan Fox — *Anne Elliot – Displaced Person?* (in *Perspectives* 79 ed. Fox & McFarlane Sorrett Publishing, Malvern, Australia 1978)

Vivien Jones — *Self and Society:* ***Persuasion*** in *How To Study A Jane Austen Novel* Macmillan Basingstoke 1987.

Penny Gay — *Visiting Mrs Smith:* ***Persuasion's*** *New Perspectives* (a lecture for the English Association, Sydney 1991)

G A Wilkes — *Autumn at Uppercross; A Note on the Use of Landscape* in ***Persuasion*** (*Sydney Studies In English* Vol 16 1990- 91)

Other Recommended Works

Joanne Wilkes — *Jane Austen's* ***Persuasion*** Horizon Studies in Literature Sydney University Press 1991

B G Southam ed. — *Jane Austen:* ***Northanger Abbey*** *And* ***Persuasion*** (Casebook) Macmillan 1976

Gillian Beer — Introduction to Penguin Classics edition *Persuasion* 1998

Viewing

BBC (Granada) TV Series 1971 adapted by Julian Mitchell, directed by Howard Baker with Ann Fairbank as Anne and Bryan Marshall as Captain Wentworth. Available ABC Shops and on Video.

FILM 1996 directed by Roger Michell with Amanda Root as Anne and Ciaran Hinds as Captain Wentworth. Available on Video.

> Obviously the TV Series, originally screened as 4 episodes of approximately 55 minutes, is longer and more detailed and includes more of Jane Austen's dialogue but the film contains most of the important plot episodes.
>
> If time permits the viewing of both versions could lead to comparisons.
>
> The following discussion points could also be used for a single viewing of either version.

a) The TV series **begins** as the novel **with Sir Walter** whereas the film **opens** – and closes – **with naval scenes.** Possible reason for this change/director's interpretation?

b) Discussion could examine how well some of the following important scenes are realised:
   - the opening scenes at Kellynch/discussion of rentrenchments.
   Is the novel's satirical tone captured?
   - Anne's first meeting with Wentworth after eight years.
   Compare narrative techniques in Chapter 7.
   - Anne at Uppercross – **How well is her emotional isolation, her sense of being an 'outsider' conveyed?** For example:
     - the Musgrove dinner party
     - Charles and Mary arguing at breakfast over which sister Wentworth prefers
     - the walk to Winthrop.
   - the scenes at Lyme.
   How well is Louisa's accident conveyed on film? Compare the novel's comic tone. Is the point of Benwick's romantic indulgence in his grief clearly made?
   - the concert in Bath.
   Are Wentworth's changing moods, Anne's anxiety to communicate, captured?

c) **Style/Mood**
   The Regency world it evokes feels scuffed and lived in. (**Newsweek**)
   Roger Michell bravely forswears glamour for understated yearning. (Claudia Johnson **Times Literary Supplement**.)
   Do these comments on the film also apply to the TV series?
   (Compare Hollywood's pretty, 'chocolate-box' **Emma**.)

d) *The camera becomes the visual equivalent of Jane Austen's rich, commenting voice* (**New York Times**)
   This comment on the film could be related to either version, discussing for example:
   - whether the **irony** of much of Austen's authorial comment is effectively conveyed;
   - whether her technique of giving the reader insight into **Anne's unspoken thoughts** translates to film/TV.

e) **Performances / Casting**
- The casting of Anne is obviously important. **How well is her gentle, self-effacing manner portrayed?**

   Amanda Root's Anne is hardly a conventional screen heroine. Plain and sad-eyed, she doesn't make much of an initial impression, which is part of Michell's strategy. Anne has been shunted off to the side of her family. She's an observer, a listener, but gradually we come to see the inner beauty that distinguishes her from her sisters. (David Ansen, *Newsweek*)

   Root's most obvious asset - her expressive eyes, which display everything from longing and pain to surprise and joy. (James Berardinelli, *Culture kiosque*)

   Could these descriptions be applied to Ann Fairbank's portrayal in the TV series?
- The *Newsweek* review praised the performance of Sir Walter (*Corin Redgrave, wonderfully loathsome*) and Mary (*the hilarious Sophie Thompson*) and the *Detroit Review* that of *the sublime Fiona Shaw as Mrs Croft, the adventurous, jolly officer's wife who by example . . . becomes a kind of role model for Anne.*

   These and other characterisations could be discussed and / or compared

f) Both versions end with a **kiss** –
- that in the BBC series in private, with the sounds of the card party in the other room as background;
- the one in the film in public, with Anne and Wentworth oblivious to the Bath street around them (the bustling crowd in Chapter 23 replaced by a parade of passing clowns, band and stilt-walkers – followed by quiet).

   Discussion might examine which is closer to the spirit of Jane Austen. (See the novel pp242-3 and top p248.)

Addendum: Alternative Page References Worksheets 1-13

The following are page references for the Penguin Classics edition (published 1998)

Worksheet 1
3. d) pp194-9;   **e)** pp202-210;   **f)** p216.

Worksheet 2
1. b) i) pp10-11;   ii) Ch 5 p32; Ch 13 p113ff; Ch 15 p124;   **c)** p36;   **d)** p30;   **e)** i) p39, pp42-3;
ii) p120-121;   **f)** p86;   **g)** p89;   **i)** Ch 17 p136; Ch 18 p148;   **j)** p15, p121;   **k)** p127.

Worksheet 3
a) p12;   **b)** ii) p230;   **c)** pp133-5, p160;   **d)** pp38-43, pp45-6; Ch 8 p58, pp60-61; Ch 7 pp49-52;
Ch 8 p64; Ch 10 pp108-9; Ch 12 pp92-3;   **e)** p22, pp61-4, p76, pp82-3, pp113-5, p145, pp150-1;
f) i) p88;   ii) p193, pp198-9;   **g)** p88, p89.

Workshheet 4
3. b) top of p19.

Worksheet 5
Group Work First Section 3. p44, p46, pp48-49, pp52-3, pp53-4;
6. References pp57-8, p61, pp64-5, pp67-70, pp71-3, pp75-6, pp78-9, p80, pp81-2, pp82-3,
p84, p88, pp93-4;   **7.** p98ff, pp102, p104;   **9. b)** p101, p104, p105 Vol 2 p113, p119;   **10.** p111;
Group Work Second Section 1. Ch 13 p110, pp113-4, p115; Ch 14 p119; Ch 18 p147, pp148-9,
p151-4; Ch 19 pp156-8, p159, p160; Ch 20 pp161-5, pp167-8, pp168-9; Ch 21 p170, p174; Ch 22
p195, p195, pp197-8, pp198-9, p200;   **2.** pp212-5; Ch 23 p202, pp203-4, pp204-7, pp208-9,
pp210-11.

Worksheet 6 (Original ending not printed in this edition.)

Worksheet 7
2. c) Ch 14 p121; Ch 15 pp124-6; Ch 14 p119, p121; Ch 16 pp131-2; Ch 17 p142, p144;
3. a) p175, pp185-6;   **3. b)** pp140-1   **4. a)** p16, pp18-20, pp30-2, p130, p141, p189;
4, b) p220, pp155-6, pp195-6, pp200-1 pp130-1.

Worksheet 9
2. pp40-1, pp51-2;   **3.** Ch 10 p78; Ch12 p98; Ch 12 p104; Ch 23 p212;   **5.** Ch 4 p24; Ch 7 p55;
Ch 17, p142; Ch20 p167; Ch 23 p214; Ch 21 p186; Ch 23 p216; Ch 24 p219

Worksheet 10
1. d) p214;   **2. a)** p213;   **b)** pp168-9;   **3. a)** p206;   **b)** p22, pp62-4, pp150.

Worksheet 11
1. b) p94, p111, p130, p158, p164, p216;   **3. b)** pp117-9, p147, pp152-3, p162, pp204-7, pp90-1,
pp96-7, p98, pp117-20, pp147-9, pp204-7;   **c)** p209, p212, p214, p212.

Worksheet 13
1. d) i) p54, p169;   **3. a)** p75, p76, p76 p77;   **c)** p156 , p159;   **d)** p168, p170.

COMPARISON QUESTIONS:
Pride and Prejudice, Emma and *Persuasion*

1. *The vivacious, intelligent Elizabeth Bennet and the confident Emma Woodhouse are very different characters from the gentle, self-effacing Anne Elliot.*
   Compare the characterisation of Anne with that of **either** Elizabeth **or** Emma. Has Austen succeeded, despite their differences, in making both sympathetic characters for a reader.

2. *In all Jane Austen's novels the heroine's qualities are illuminated by being set against those of other female characters.*
   Discuss this idea in relation to two novels (refer to at least two characters as well as the heroine herself).

3. *In all Jane Austen's novels the heroine is involved with a charming 'villain'.*
   Compare the uses made of these men in *Pride and Prejudice, Emma* and *Persuasion*. (You will need to discuss other male characters as well.)

4. *Despite the focus on heroine and hero, minor characters in Austen's novels are important in presenting her main concerns.*
   Discuss this proposition, referring in detail to **at least two** novels.

5. *She shows herself to be a shrewd observer of the comic possibilities of human nature – the foibles and weaknesses, the inconsistencies and self-deceptions shown by most people.*
   Examine Austen's use of these 'comic possibilities of human nature' in **at least two** novels.

6. *"What incomparable noodles she exhibits for our astonishment and laughter!"* (G H Lewes)
   Which of Jane Austen's comic characters do you find most amusing? Why? (Use **at least two** novels.)

7. A C Bradley identified our pleasure in reading Jane Austen with the fact that *she regards all her characters, good and bad alike, with ironical amusement, because they never see the situation as it really is and as she sees it.*
   Does this apply equally well to *Persuasion* as to Pride and Prejudice or Emma?

8. *It has been said that Jane Austen's novels are basically about marriage and money but her 'good' characters never marry in a heartless, exploitative fashion without love.*
   Test this by discussing the treatment of courtship and marriage in **at least two** novels.

9. *The limitations placed upon women by her society and the possibility of happiness for an intelligent or sensitive woman in that society is a concern throughout Jane Austen's novels.*
   Show whether you agree with this idea by a discussion of **two or three** novels.

10. *"entertaining studies of her society and its trivial doings presented with amused tolerance."*
    "a dislike of the society depicted, often conveyed in passing, occasionally intense and bitter"
    Which of these attitudes to her world and its values do you find in Jane Austen's novels? (Support your argument by detailed reference to **at least two** novels.